GLOW IN THE DARK

GOOD MORNING – I WONDER – HEARD 'EM SAY – THROUGH THE WIRE – CHAMPION – GET 'EM HIGH – DIAMONDS FROM SIERRA LEONE – CAN'T TELL ME NOTHING – FLASHING LIGHTS – SPACESHIP – ALL FALLS DOWN – GOLD DIGGER – GOOD LIFE – JESUS WALKS – HEY, MAMA – DON'T STOP BELIEVIN' – STRONGER – HOMECOMING – TOUCH THE SKY

First published in the United States of America in 2009
by Rizzoli International Publications, Inc.
300 Park Avenue South
New York, New York 10010
www.rizzoliusa.com

© 2008 Kanye West and Nabil Elderkin

Photography by Nabil Elderkin
with the exception of:
Pages 94–95 original artwork, model, and design
by Es Devlin
Pages 118–119 images courtesy ARTBEATS
Gatefold "Fuck Kanye" port-a-potty photograph by
Alexander Hazel © 2008 Kanye West
Pages 6, 10, 28–29, 64–65 (angel image courtesy
Mia Okorafor c/o AMCK), and 100
photography and artwork © 2008 Simon Henwood,
Production Director and Designer/
European leg of Glow in the Dark tour
Page 83 sketches courtesy Jim Henson Studios
Pages 84–86 and 96–97 photography © 2008
Tobias Spellman
J.A.N.E. spaceship and globe design featured on U.S.
leg of tour © 2008 Martin Phillips (see page 152)
Plastic doll with blue hair featured on U.S. leg of
tour © 2008 Colin Christian (see page 152)
Pages 258–259 © 2008 MTV Networks Europe.
All Rights Reserved.
Page 102 image used with permission of
Madison Square Garden

Vanessa Beecroft, 2008
VBKW (Kanye West performance)
Ace Gallery, Los Angeles, CA
Pages 217–219 (images vbkw.04.jm, vbkw.01.jm,
vbkw.02.jm, and vbkw.10.jm) photography
by John Maxwell
Page 220 (images vbkw.011.jj, vbkw.012.jj,
vbkw.013.jj, vbkw.014.jj, vbkw.015.jj, and
vbkw.016.jj) photography by Jesper Justesen
Light Design by Jonathan Goldstein
© Vanessa Beecroft 2009

Design by BASE

Edited by Leah Whisler, Art Directed by Ian Luna

2009 2010 2011 2012 2013 / 10 9 8 7 6 5 4 3 2 1

Printed in China

Trade ISBN: 978-0-8478-3240-8
Library of Congress Catalog Control Number: 2009923599

Deluxe ISBN: 978-0-8478-3294-1
Library of Congress Catalog Control Number: 2009923604

CD tracks, courtesy Universal Music, Roc-A-Fella Records,
and Island Def Jam.

"I Wonder" remix
Contains elements of "My Song" written by Labi Siffre M.A.M.
(Music Publishing) Corp. (ASCAP) All Rights Administered
by Chrysalis Music. All Rights Reserved. Courtesy EMI
Blackwood Music, Inc.; Please Gimme My Publishing, Inc.
Writers: Labi Siffre and Kanye West.

"Jesus Walks" remix
Courtesy Che Smith and Curtis Lundy
EMI Blackwood Music, Inc.; Please Gimme My Publishing, Inc.
Universal Music MG songs obo Solomon Ink. Writers: Curtis
Lundy, Che Smith, and Kanye West. All Rights Reserved.

"Hey Mama" remix
Courtesy Very Every Music; EMI Blackwood Music, Inc.;
Please Gimme My Publishing, Inc. Writers: Donal Richard
Leace and Kanye West. All Rights Reserved.

"Touch the Sky" remix
Courtesy Universal Music; Heaven as Heaven Music, EMI
Blackwood Music, Inc.; Please Gimme My Publishing, Inc.;
Warner-Tamerlane Pub Corp; N.Q.C. Music Publishing; F.O.B.
Music Publishing. Samples "Move on Up." Writers: Wasalu
Jaco, Justin Smith, Mayfield Curtis, and Kanye West. All
Rights Reserved.

GLOW IN THE DARK

KANYE WEST

CONTENTS

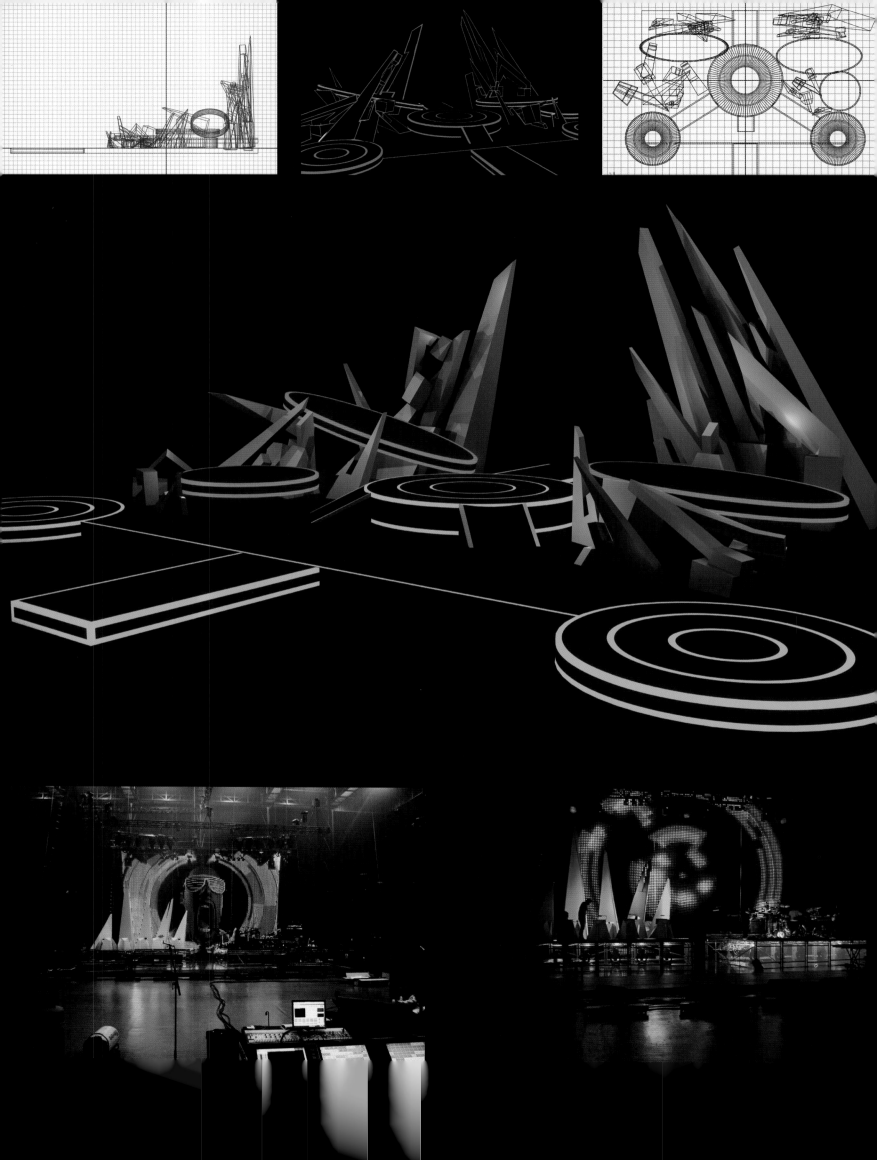

INTERVIEW WITH
KANYE WEST & SPIKE JONZE

KANYE WEST: [Singing.] It's amazing, amazing. I love going through this book, because it brings back so many memories.

SPIKE JONZE: You've done tours before; why did you want to capture this one in a book?

We were videoing it and getting photographed because all types of amazing, cool stuff happens to me every day, and I was, like, "I'm doing an interview with Spike today; what did *you* do?" It was good to document it. Then it just so happened to be so cultural and visually amazing. I'll [also] explain once we go from the European tour, and the different stuff that inspired me to completely throw everything out the window and come up with the U.S. tour, the one that you saw. And you have a bit of back story because you were helping to conceptualize some of the stuff for the tour.

Personally, what does this tour mean? And what's it going to feel like for you to have it in a book?

It's just an emotional time, I think, for everybody in the world, dealing with change. It was all about change and graduation: my first year into my thirties, the losses I was dealing with—my mother, my relationship. And making a conscious effort to not allow people's perceptions of what I was or what I was supposed to do take my freedom away from me because that's what it is: people try to box you in and take your freedom away. I refused to let that happen. I made a conscious effort to say, I'm going to be a creative individual; I'll just deal with the backlash—people who are scared to change and grow, which is what life is about. I think [documenting this tour was] more interesting than me getting a record deal, winning the Grammys, and the obvious things that people would've made a movie about. Like, you're stepping into doing, not a by-fluke thing, not a one-off, first-album thing, not a first-time-at-the-Grammys thing, but a true artist at war with his self and the world and emotions—the fight to be creative, to keep from thinking about how much fucked-up shit was happening to me. I had to be creative to keep my mind off of it.

That's what you used your work for that year?

I didn't realize; I just did it. I worked constantly instead of thinking about what I was actually going through. In hindsight, I'm like, "Wow, this meant this, this meant that."

What was the expectation for you before you did this tour?

Specifically, the expectation for the tour was way lower than what I presented. I love to present art that's different, that might be polarizing, that might jar you, but then surpasses your expectations. Like when we watched this [*Where the Wild Things Are* clip] right now, and I said, "Oh, wow, this is completely different than I thought; this way surpasses my expectation of the amount of dialogue that the Wild Things had." I thought they were just going to be kind of scary, grunting, *grr*, but it's like a Woody Allen movie.

You were working on your second record when I first met you, and people were looking at you like you were competing with 50 Cent or Jay-Z. You said, "I don't look at myself as competing with them. I'm not competing with rap; I'm competing with Madonna, and I'm competing with Michael Jackson, and I'm competing with Prince—that's what I'm aiming for."

Until I beat them; then I'll find someone else to compete with. You've got to be grateful for artists like Lil Wayne—people who can push you and inspire you and give you something to beat in the morning—because otherwise it's like playing basketball by yourself. Beyoncé was hooping by herself until Rihanna came in and got on the other side of the court and started hitting some shots. Then Beyoncé's, like, "Oh, man, I'm going to have to come

with it; I'm going to drop "Single Ladies" and just drop the best video ever of all time."

So *Graduation* and the tour, as a moment in your life—what do you think you transitioned into through the course of that year and a half?

Well, it's weird—to segue off of what you were saying about the competition with me and 50—I'm definitely David and everyone else is Goliath. Even if I'm the biggest, I'm always going to raise someone else up as Goliath, put someone else on the court. I'll play centers and stuff, I'll play point guards, I'll play whoever I have to play, but I like the concept of competition. I think that's 50; he kind of built off competition, but his method of attack was more brutal than psychological. My thing is more like fighting water with fire; just figuring how to beat the big boss at the end, not by shooting him right in his chest but maybe in some way running around the side of his leg, hitting him on the shin—that's how you beat that game.

Might have to work harder, be more clever.

You've got to rely on what your end goal is. Society and culture have presented options, then you figure out what options apply to you and which don't. For me, the option of Christianity doesn't apply to me, even though that's what I was taught. So now it's a major thing that's coming out, like, "Dude, he doesn't believe in Jesus." It's crazy. Someone could be a straight killer and talk about murdering people and do all these bad things, and they'll say, "Oh, God, I'm sorry," and everybody's, like, "That's cool." Someone could put out mad positive energy, beautiful art—everything—and just help so many people, then say, "Yo, you know, I don't believe in Jesus, though." Then it's, like, "Whoa, he's a bad person."

How did that relate to the battle...from David and Goliath? I might've just spaced out for a second, what the connection was.

Okay, it's a battle. I also, like, rant into other information. The connection is the battle within yourself—the battle of your image. I'm at battle with the media, people's perception of me, versus me. So many people have this perception of me. I look like a really big piece of shit to them, for whatever reason, then they get up close and they're, like, "Wow, this is not a piece of shit; this has good in it. This is really good."

I think you're easy to quote, and those quotes are easy to take out of context. You just say whatever you're thinking, which I love. Some things you say sound egomaniacal when you take them out of context, and especially out of the context of the big picture of who you are. I liked when you said, "I'm a fan of anything that's great. If the new Yeah Yeah Yeahs' record comes out and I love it, I'm a fan of theirs. If Murakami has something new that I love, I'm a fan of it. And if *I* make something that I love, then I'm going to be a fan of it. I'm not going to be falsely humble." I don't know what the solution is, because it's what makes an article, it's the thing they report on. They say the most sensationalistic thing you said, without any of the nuance—

And giving any context to it.

You were saying at one point that was part of why you wanted to start the blog—

It's like when you're picking out new clothes and stuff that you might not be used to, that looks crazy. Sometimes it takes a stylist to put it into context. Basically, my quotes are like a bunch of crazy clothes laid out there in the middle of the street.

Uh-huh. [Laughs.]

My biggest thing is clarity. I wish people could understand where

I'm coming from. So many people are scared; they'd rather just fit into what society says. You know it's going to be taken out of context if you say something good about yourself, so just never say anything good about yourself. Never say that you believe in you. I refuse to fit into what society thinks I should be doing because, at the end of the day, it's my life.

Bringing us back to *Graduation* and this tour, what was the expectation you were battling against?

I don't know. Last year was one of the few times it seemed like people were on my side, because they didn't like 50. They wanted to pick somebody, like, "Oh, he's the lesser of two evils" or something. There was a brief moment when people actually felt for me—two weeks that I got a pass—then it's, like, "Yo, back to 'Fuck you, Kanye.'" Now everything I say, they feel like it's because I've grown crazy because of the situations I've been through—my mom passing or the relationship that I got out of. It's not that I've gone crazy; I just don't feel like I have anything to lose, so I might as well express exactly what I feel. It's like the everyday version of someone in their final argument in a relationship.

With who?

With anyone. When you talk to me, I'm going to be as open as your girlfriend is that last argument. It's just super-real, this is how I actually really feel. Every day, though. And that's really awkward for people.

Have you been that way from day one, or do you think you're growing into that even more?

I'm growing to accept the ups and downs of it and not be so frustrated by the backlash. I'm going to say, this is how I feel. I'd rather piss a bunch of people off and be happy with myself than have a whole bunch of people happy and be pissed at myself.

For not being true to yourself.

For not being true. That's the most important thing to me, to be true to me.

Why does that piss people off, do you think? Because, actually, I haven't heard a lot of Kanye shit-talking, lately.

Like maybe people are understanding me a bit more or something?

When I left that concert, people were so happy, in the best mood. They got everything they wanted and more. There was a real positive—

Yeah, it's like when Kobe wins a championship, they're super happy, happy to be in L.A. and, "We love Kobe so much." Certain types of individuals say too much of anything is bad. It may be bad for you, like, have you worked too much on your movie?

Probably.

Any true artist is going to do it too much. That's what I do; I am an expert at doing too much, overdoing it, OCD, being in the studio too long. Who's to say what's good and bad? "Oh, but too much religion is not good, or too much church is not good, or too much working out is not good." Society has its things they feel are good and bad. If you buy too many gym shoes, that's a good thing, but if you buy, like, too much porn, that's a bad thing. So what I keep stressing is, I'm not going to let someone else dictate the amount of what I should have. I know what feels right in my spirit. I know when I get a stomachache because I ate too much ice cream. I know when I look fat in the mirror, because I've just been eating a bunch of fried chicken, and I make the decision of whether or not I want to eat less.

o you feel like you have your own radar when you feel like a healthy, ositive person, and you like yourself.

That's where my radar is right now, more than ever. I used to be nsecure, I used to be scared. I'm just not scared. I'm not scared o die. I'm not scared to talk. I'm not scared to communicate. I'm ot scared to deliver my art in the purest form I want to deliver it. When we did "Flashing Lights," a bunch of people said, "Man, you eed to show a club scene." That was my favorite video to date. t expressed exactly what I wanted to express, the exact type of isuals that meant something to me. I feel like I have the best taste. Laughs.] Other people have really good taste, and I'll bow in their resence and listen to them and say, "Maybe I haven't focused as uch on Telecine, so I'm going to let you do the knobs and stuff." know it's basically what I want to see at the end of the day. I'm ot trying to build a car; I'm not an expert at that. But if you talk to ne about something that I'm an expert at, I'm going to be super-onfident about it. If I have a doctor working on me, I want the nost confident doctor possible. I don't want somebody up there, stuttering] "I-I-I-I don't know what I'm doing." Our lives are novies, and I'm providing the soundtrack. I would only hope that ou would want somebody confident to provide that for you. When ou look back twenty years from now, you listened to a song that vas done by an expert, versus like some accidental bullshit where ou're, like, "Man, I can't believe I was listening to that." Be happy hat you have that expert building the score to your life.

like that you've reached a place where you're fearless.

wouldn't say completely fearless, because that's delusional. Confidence, courage, isn't not having fear, but being able o overcome that. More than anything, I'm courageous. I'm ourageous to say the things I'm saying, knowing the type of acklash I can get from it. You have to be courageous just to be ourself. Whenever you see somebody completely be who they re, you have to love that. I love when people are super-religious, ecause that's who they are. I, every day, remove another layer of nobbery.

ou have? Because you used to have more snobbery for people who vere—

used to just not like people who weren't into what I was into, which s the way the average person is. If you're doing something negative, ow, I can't fully accept that. I could say, "Dude, you're wack. I'm ot into it. You're about doing negative stuff, putting out negative nergy. Fuck you, I don't like that." But if you're doing something hat makes you feel good, that I might not be into, then hey—

it's not hurting anybody else, yeah.

hat's cool for me. If it's cool with you, you like it, I love it.

What about failure? Before you make a record that's popular, you don't ave anything to lose. Now that you've made three or four records that re huge, do you worry about following your instincts so far that they take ou away from popular success?

Whenever I get worried about something, I just remind myself that have to look at it and know if *I* like it or not. The biggest thing is to e off. Once you're off with culture and society, once you're in a lace where it's like you don't understand why people like stuff... ke, I understand why people like Ed Hardy. If I can be in tune with hat most people like, that's the great talent. At the end of the ay, everything about me is taste level and collaging. I collage— pping, rhyming, with information that my father's given me about ulture and society—then I make songs like "All Falls Down" then ollage the information I've got about producing, that I've learned om this one, and put it all together. You're sitting there, you're ooking at ten pictures, you take two pictures from here, then you ook at [another] ten pictures and take two pictures from there, and hose two pictures that you take is your taste level. So good taste is hat it is. I'm a little snobby towards schmuckery, you know.

ait, what's schmuckery?

chmuckery, schmucks.

ke people being dicks to other people, or work that is shitty?

eah, people who just put out shitty work. I'd be more apt to be business with a character like you than—I'm not going to name omebody, but—other types of people in Hollywood who might ave this hit movie after hit movie. That's not my gang. I don't it for the check. I'm super happy at the end of the day. I'm omfortable with where I'm at. I'm not as rich as anyone who's entioned in the same breath as me in entertainment. I think I've assed up on some checks, just for the ability to be me.

ke what kind of checks? Endorsement deals, or—?

aybe it's certain endorsements, maybe it's certain licenses, aybe it's certain, "Shut the fuck up, don't say how you feel, that

brand of anybody, because I'd still like to do business with them. I'm not turning the check down, but just to say—

I'm from the outside; I'm trying to figure out why you wouldn't be as rich, because it seems like your records are huge, your tours are huge—

I'm not saying things to be polarizing, I'm saying things because I really feel like they are the absolute right. My biggest thing is to bring the same people who did the Daft Punk tour to a pop tour—for people to see dope shit. That's one of my main goals. I want really great, maybe more obscure at the time, artists to be seen on a pop level, because I would say that one of my religions is pop. I subscribe to pop culture. So, in that way, I believe in the Bible. I'll quote the Bible all day long because it's the most popular thing to quote. It's all about communication and people understanding you. Disney—what was so great about that is it was pop and it was also better than everything else. That's what I want, the type of music I want to make. Beyoncé—it's good that she's coming up with stuff that's blatantly better than independent artists. She's Beyoncé. I think that's kind of what the recession is about, too; there's no in-between at all. If you're really, really good, people will still be, like, "Okay, I'm in the store, I can only buy one CD, and this is what I'm going to buy."

You were talking about collaging. What would you say are the biggest influences in your work, in your career, up to date, that made you who you are?

My biggest influences were my parents now, after the fact. When you're in high school, you'd love to say that your parents aren't the ones influencing you, it's the people around you. But my parents and television and media—my face is definitely stuck to that TV. I wanted to get into the TV. Like *Poltergeist*. And I managed to do it. Now I'm in the little box. Television and media are my biggest influences; that's also one of the reasons I get so upset when the media tries to influence people to not like me, try to "Mel Gibson" me or something. It would be a shame if someone didn't watch *Apocalypto* because of how they felt about Mel Gibson. It's just, arguably, one of the top ten movies of all time. His work is so amazing.

I haven't seen that movie yet.

Oh, my God. It will influence you, because it's all action, back-to-back. It's the most amazing action movie ever made. But it's not in English. It has subtitles—an action movie with all subtitles. You think subtitles, you think drama or something. What's a shame is that there are people who, because of their beliefs, might not listen to my music, might not come to a concert. But, at the end of the day, there's only 20,000 seats in the arena, and we sold 'em all out, so—what can you do? [Laughter.]

So who were you when you started this tour, and who were you when you ended it?

Man, let's talk about this tour life. I'm way closer to the person I was at age five than I was five years ago—just refinding yourself, finding your child, having the opportunity to be a child; that's the greatest thing, because people force you to be adult. We're two of the few people on earth who have the full right to be kids. My dancing is so bad that I do onstage, I refuse to look at the playback on it, because it would change the way I dance the next day.

Inhibit you or something. That's what's so great about Karen [of the Yeah Yeah Yeahs]—she is tapped into that kid feeling. She's totally guileless and free, and a total kid onstage. It's hard to keep that when you hear a lot of people judging you or talking about you. How do you tap in—?

How do you block out the judgment? That's why I feel so empowered. It might upset me a bit when I'm judged, but I can use it as fuel to get better, to prove people wrong and still focus on what it is I want to do. I'm going to do it my way, and you're going to like it, even when you didn't like it at first.

How do you think this tour helped you get back to being a five-year-old?

Well, just being on that stage, hopping up and down, dancing like crazy. An interesting thing about the design of this is, I was definitely in a position where we had already sold tickets—this U.S. tour's finally going to be here, it's the biggest album in the country. I had to go on tour, but it's definitely a time where I shouldn't have been. I should've taken a vacation; I should've just did what I wanted to do. I had a car accident—before the major one that everyone knows about. My truck flipped over. It was such a life-altering thing that you just go back into that childhood state. They have movies when something happens, you're about to die, your life flashes before your eyes. So, after my life flashing before my eyes—that car accident—I went to my apartment and set up a race-car track right in the middle of the living room. I sat there for hours and hours and just raced cars. When you're at work, don't you ever just feel like, "Damn, I wish I was just racing cars—back when it was Christmas, at age seven..."

When I was a child, and watched sci-fi films, I used to take my mom's bed sheets—she had this one quilt that was blue on one side and white on the other, and I would take it and flip it to the white sid and put pillows under it to recreate the planets in the movies. I wou set all my characters up on it and be one of the characters. If you really think about it, that's exactly what my stage was. When thing are truly inspired and meant to be, and they just flow through you i some way, the true inspiration for that was that childhood that cam through me, where I was, like, "I have to tour, and I don't want to!" But if I'm going to do it, then I'm going to dress up like a spaceman. When I was in kindergarten, they did these tests and they had me draw, and I was, like, "Can I draw a football player?" And they were like, "No, just draw a regular guy." I was, like, "Okay, I'm going to draw a regular guy, but I'm going to put a football player outfit on him." This was my response as a kindergartner. I'm mature now, but I'm still going to flip that bed sheet over and try to make a snow planet.

I love it. That's awesome. So let's start at the beginning. Who took the photos?

Nabil Elderkin. And he's going to be a big, famous photographer after this comes out.

So it was basically two tours. The first one, where it was a little less focused, and the second, where you just threw it all out and started over.

Yeah. But the first tour was good; it had its thing, too.

What was it? I didn't see that one.

There were people who said they liked that tour better, even. I originally sat down with Jamie King, because I was idolizing Madonna, and he's a choreographer who's worked with Madonna.

Is he a tour or set designer?

He's just an overall visual creator-director. But it would be so expensive, because you had to pay him, and he'd go hire other creative people, then hire the stage person, then hire the video guys—the price would just go way up. I ended up meeting with this guy Simon Henwood, who's Roisin Murphy's boyfriend—I saw this Roisin Murphy video that I thought was genius, and I wanted to sit and talk to him about doing a video.

Who's Roisin Murphy?

Roisin Murphy is, I guess her music could be considered pop, but she's very edgy, she's really fashionable. She was wearing Margiela shoulder pads, she's like the poster child for that. She changes outfits like ten times onstage. Her band and visuals are extremely great. I think she's a genius, and her boyfriend is a genius, too. He ended up doing the "Love Lockdown" video, then, a year and a half afterwards, we started getting cool. I sat with him to talk about videos. Whenever I'm sitting with a creative person, I'll start bouncing all types of ideas off of them, because you can create in an space. How do we apply this genius to this, to this, to this? So we enc up starting to think of two ideas. I remember also sitting with Dave LaChapelle, because I really loved the Elton John thing he had done

Right. I remember you showed me some clips on YouTube of this half of the tour. So what do you call the first half?

It was called Glow in the Dark.

Glow in the Dark Europe, then Glow in the Dark U.S.? Is that how you differentiate between the two sections?

No, because then I had to skip back and forth. By the time we got to Asia, we had to go back to a hybrid of the first set, then we'd do different one-offs, and it would be a hybrid of the original set.

Because you couldn't travel the whole thing through Asia?

Yeah, I couldn't have the stage.

I know from friends who go on tour that, for the two hours of life onstage, the other twenty-two hours are much less glamorous.

The backstage, car service, and airport—like a circus act. You choose the people you want to tour with, but then you have to be around them for fifty days!

I've heard it mentioned that it's like *Groundhog Day*: the hotels all look the same; the airport looks the same; the car looks the same; the backstage looks the same. You're not even really traveling, because you don't get to—

Yeah, thank god for the Internet now, because people used to play video games a lot before the Internet.

Before we go into this, tell the story of Glow in the Dark, Part II, with J.A.N.E.—briefly, from the top.

rumbling, and I explain to the audience—I did it live; I could have pre-recorded it, but I did it live—that "I've been on this mission to bring creativity back to the earth…" because the wells are dried up and this is our last mission before we head home. We're about to head home, then me and J.A.N.E. hit a meteor shower and, as the meteor shower starts, these big taiko drums end up going into this "Stronger" intro. We end up crash-landing on this planet. The first time you see me, I'm laying on my back, which I think is great because I always play off people's perception of me. To have me laid out on my back as the antihero was a way cooler intro than me coming out like, "Yeah, I'm Kanye. Look at me. I got an explosion behind me." I wake up and my spaceship starts talking to me, and the first thing you hear is her say, "Wake up, Mr. West." When we do the meteor shower, she's, like, "We are approaching a meteor shower. Caution. We've been hit. Emergency." You know, that type of shit. And it's like [makes noise] the taiko drums. So I wake up then do "Good Morning." Then I talk to the spaceship, and I'm, like, "Where are we?" She says, "Unfortunately, Mr. West, we have crash-landed on an unknown planet." I'm, like, "Where are we?" She says, "Unknown." I'm, like, "How long will it take to get fixed?" She says, "Unknown." I'm, like, "J.A.N.E., what are we going to do?" And she's, like, "Unknown." I'm, like "Ahhhh!" Then it goes into "I Wonder," because what are we going to do? "I wonder, if you know, what it means…[sings]." I do that and that's the first time you kind of see the screen just go full-on and stuff.

So redoing the set—throwing the whole set out—I'm sure that must have cost a lot of money. Were you able to still make money doing the tour?

It cost millions of dollars, or something like that, but yeah, I still made some money at the end of the day—maybe half of what I would've made. I'm more concerned about the fans—that money that I lost, I'm going to make up for on my next tour. I feel like everybody's going to be like, "We have to see what this dude is going to come up with now. We trust this"—like how you start to trust the album. There are no acts from this genre of music that you trust their touring—that you're like, "Oh, my God, this is going to be the most amazing tour." Even if you didn't like anything off 808s & Heartbreak, you'd still go just to see how I do "Stronger" this time.

Are you going to tour 808s & Heartbreak?

I was thinking about just touring 808s & Heartbreak, because I'm a fucking weirdo who's doing a theater tour. So if they go, "Yo, do 'Gold Digger,'" I'm, like, "Fuck you." [Laughter.]

Back to this tour—I think it just had great energy. That's what's so great about something live.

[Looking at photos of book.] But I also think a photo captures the emotion sometimes better than a DVD, depending on how it was shot. Look at how massive the screen looks behind me. To be so diligent and sticking to the plan with the screens. The screens never show me really big.

The screen was the set.

I don't think there's ever been anyone—no rock star—who didn't decide, at some point, to put themselves up on the screen really big. It's, like, [doing a rockstar impression] "I need to see myself." There were so many things that—for me to be such a so-called arrogant dude—that I just didn't do. Like I never put myself on the album cover. My shit is just more about trying to create the best art possible.

I remember afterwards thinking how intense it was that you were going full-on for two hours, and thinking you must be dead every night. What was it like giving it up for two hours by yourself on a stage that big?

It was a workout, and my breathing, my voice, and the amount of energy I'm putting out—it was very emotional because of the things I was going through when I would do certain songs. Especially towards the end—by the time the newness of all the ideas was wearing off and it was time to think about new ideas—it became more routine. At that point, I was forced to think about real life again, and about the sadness of where I was and where I am—what I'm trying to get over. I went from not having talked to my mom for three months to not having talked to her for a year, and still being on that same stage.

What were some of the hardest shows?

The absolute hardest show for me was Brazil. You'd think that would be a dream come true for me, to be in Brazil. But I was having arguments with someone, and it just made me feel like I was really alone on that stage. When I was performing "The Good Life" in Brazil, I would actually be crying because of the irony of that song, like "welcome to this good life." Plus, things were going wrong, and we had a different lighting guy for that show and—it's like when everything goes right, sometimes you can zone out and just be in this euphoria; everything is all good; you can get rocked to sleep. But then if you have a really bad day, you start

looking up at everything and being, like, "What the fuck is wrong with your shoes?" and "Don't you owe me some money?" and just start thinking about everything that's wrong.

Back to this year and the tour—it seemed like it also happened over the course of the election—of Obama starting to be talked about for president until he's the Democratic candidate—and now he's president. Do you feel like, culturally, there's something going on that you're a part of—talking about race in America. Do you feel a difference?

It's a change of the guards, and my goal, to be like this first black stadium guy, to make this music, like "Stronger"—a song that blatantly rips across every station, that's not just an urban thing, it's a world thing—and at the same time for Barack to be the first in his position doing that? Yeah, it's interesting. What's also interesting is Barack listens to my music. He knows a couple songs; he's never been to a concert. I like Barack. I've heard a couple of his speeches; I mean, I finally went to the DNC. But it's a thing where it's, like, I really appreciate what he's doing, what he's about to do. And I think he also appreciates that I'm doing what I do—that my thing is not, like, "Oh, now that he's about to be a politician, I'm, all of a sudden, so into politics." Me saying that is almost equal to me being, like, "I don't believe in Jesus." It's, like, "Dude, you're not going to show up at every single thing that Barack is doing?" It's, like, "No, because I have to go to the studio, and, like, work on the soundtrack for our lives." I have to do my job. Even right now, when they're talking about the inauguration, like, "I know you're going to be at the inauguration, Kanye West," I'm, like, "I really want to be at the Prada show." In Italy. I think I'm going to be there. I'm very happy. [Laughter.]

Are you performing at the inauguration or before the inauguration?

I might be performing at the inauguration. But I really want to be at the Prada show.

Because politics aren't that important to you?

I don't care about politics. I care about clothes; I care about high hats and snares. And it's good that that's what I care about, because I do a good job at what I care about. I don't feel any type of guilt in any way, to not care about what I don't care about. I don't feel guilty that there are a lot of athletes I wouldn't recognize at a party. Back when I used to want to play basketball, I had hoop dreams; I knew every basketball player in the league. I'm not into it anymore. I don't give a fuck. So many people are, like, "Man, you need to know about this," you know? Don't you have friends who are basically like walking versions of Google?

Definitely.

I am so down to not know about everything. I don't read. Whatsoever.

You read the Internet, right? It seems like from your blog you're tapped into a lot of shit going on.

Just shit that I'm into.

It's this very specific line that surrounds what you're interested in, and if it falls outside of that—

Then I'm not interested in it.

It's off your radar.

It's off my radar. And it's on someone else's radar, and that's good for them. I'm completely fine to not know what they're doing in the back at Jamba Juice. I'm cool. I sip the juice, and that's how I feel about politics. I feel like it's in the back of Jamba Juice, and everybody feels like they need to be so involved. I'm just cool like, "Just make the juice, dude. Cool."

Maybe, at some point in your life, you will care what happens in the back of Jamba Juice or with politics.

Then I will. Or maybe I won't. Maybe I'll care about just raising my kids. Maybe that will be my focus. Politics is a hobby.

Well, it's a hobby, but it's also something that truly affects our lives. It's not like it's just happening over here. What's happening over here affects our lives, affects the world, affects policy that profoundly affects the lives of everyone in the world. It's not what's happening behind Jamba Juice. I'm not saying you have to care, but I'm saying it does affect your life—

Yeah, it's like when the Bulls won, that really affected Chicago in a positive way. The Bulls won in Chicago; that affected us. There are times when they've lost, when people rioted, and that affected us. That's how I feel. A lot of people feel like, because I'm this big figure, it's this responsibility I have to take. All I keep stressing to people is, I'm not going to take any more responsibility because I over-take responsibilities in my craft. I'm completely fine with sounding like a dumbass or being considered irresponsible in everything, because that beat turned out really good, and this

is what I do. I'm like the blue collar of whatever it is I'm into. You know what I'm saying? When you think about blue-collar workers, that's like their trade, and they're just really, really good at that. If they can't play basketball, you're not mad at them. If they're not really into politics, you're not mad at them. If your sink was clogged, and the plumber came over and fixed it, would you say, "Hey, man, how do you feel about politics? Who you voting on?" and he gave the wrong answer or said, "I don't care" or just shrugged his shoulders, would your sink be any less unclogged?

I totally agree that it's not a celebrity responsibility—

It's like Katrina, when all the celebrities were going down. I went down to Katrina afterwards and bought houses and stuff, but we did absolutely no press on it. I mean, to each his own. Maybe that was their thing, to show how much they cared, but—

It is a totally twisted culture; it does bring attention to a subject that needs to be talked about, but it's definitely a totally fucked-up society that it has to be done that way.

And, yeah, this actor—I say, "What the fuck makes that person more special?" What I want people to really realize about the Katrina thing is, I am purely a little kid. I walked in, I'm looking at that shit, and this is what a four-year-old would say. It doesn't make the four-year-old the next day not want to just go and play basketball, or "Now I want to just watch politics every day." Afterwards, I'm, like, "I'm going to go play basketball now." And it's like, "Whoa! No, you're supposed to be at every single convention from now on, because you said this one thing." It's almost like some Forrest Gump stuff for me.

You know what's crazy? When I talked to you about this, I hadn't actually seen the clip. Just in the last six months, I saw it on YouTube. I watched it, and the thing that hit me the most is how you look almost like you're about to cry. You look so nervous and like you don't know what you're saying. You're kind of just saying this stuff off the top of your head, and you're rambling, and in this world where everybody goes off cue cards, and so polished and political, and says just the right thing that won't be taken out of context, and this whole thing was just so raw, and I loved it. I loved how heartfelt it was. You were really just speaking from your heart, and that's one of the things I admire about you.

I'm like a Will Ferrell character in real life. It's like the real version of Step Brothers or something, or Ricky Bobby [Talladega Nights].

I didn't see that movie. Are they stunted?

It seems like they're complete idiots, but really they just speak exactly what they feel. There's little baby Tourette's going on.

That's what part I tried to capture in the movie [Where the Wild Things Are]—that kids are not politically correct. They say, "I'm going to kill you," "Die!" "Look at that fat guy over there." They don't think anything; they'll just say it because they haven't been taught when you're supposed to do this and society says you're supposed to do that. I could see the comparison. How do you maintain that? How do you stay spontaneous?

How do you keep your childhood and stuff? I don't know. Every day, it's an emotional and mental workout. It's similar to Pamela Anderson or somebody, keeping their body. Because their body—at a young age, they're just like young and eighteen, just the shit. Then the older you get, the more things wear on what made you purely the shit and you have to work out—work at just being you. I feel like I'm in the best shape of my life. I had a couple times where I got out of shape—a little politically correct and shit—and now I'm like a hundred thousand percent politically incorrect. I will a hundred thousand percent be at the Prada show while the inauguration is going on. I'm going to be like, "Man, those are some really nice shoes." They've inspired me in some way. There's inspiration I get from Barack, just hearing him speak, seeing the way he can compel people. I enjoy watching Barack. He's an amazing character.

Amazing, powerful speaker, who just connects.

That's what I love the most—his communication skills. His communication skills are obviously better than mine, because if he's saying what he feels—

So you're going to be, like, "I'm competing with Barack Obama now." You already went for Madonna, now you're going for Barack Obama.

I'd like my songs to communicate. There is a certain competition in politics and music and stuff. What resonates more, Stevie Wonder's "Happy Birthday" song or Dr. King's "I have a dream" speech? Do you remember the entire speech, or do you remember an entire song? What's embedded? What are the things that will flash before your eyes when you're passing away? What things are you going to remember? I guess that's my goal, to be a part of that memory, like, when you look back years from now, "I remember this right here."

GLOW IN THE DARK

PART I

BRIGHTON, UNITED KINGDOM
11.22.2007 – 11.28.2007

Simon Henwood designed these masks for the string players. They actually sat in these pyramids like the Muppets.

THIS SPREAD AND FOLLOWING Preparing to go onstage at various U.K. performance halls.

THIS PAGE, BELOW LEFT Tobias Spellman shooting footage for the concert DVD. Toby captured my whole life that year on film. BELOW RIGHT Making last-minute changes to my set list.

OPPOSITE String players dressed in costumes designed by Simon Henwood. I got the idea to place my musicians in a space below the stage after Es Devlin took me to one of the operas she set designed for.

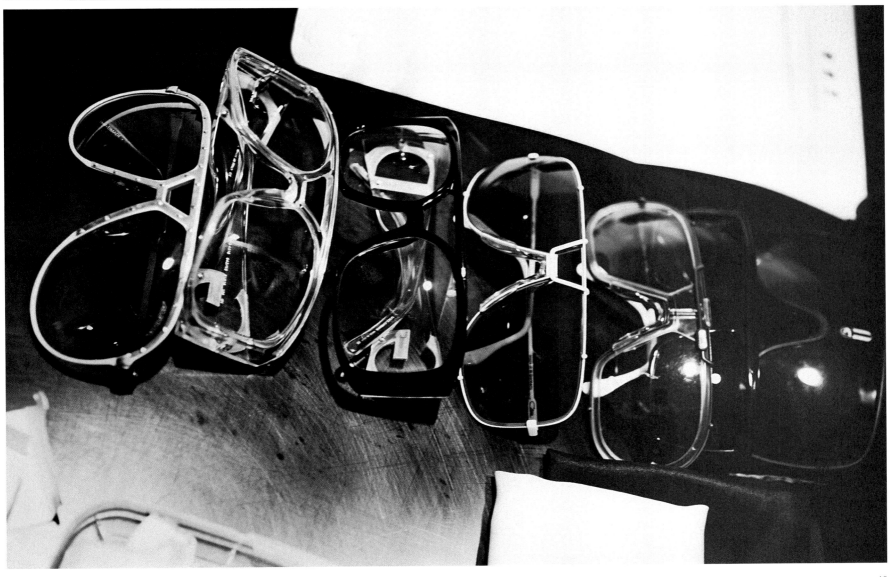

OPPOSITE Being shuttled to arena. THIS PAGE TOP Going over set list with lighting director John Goldstein [in white shirt], music director Adam Blackstone [in white hat], and crew. THIS PAGE BOTTOM Working on my outfit for "Stronger."

FOLLOWING SPREADS Onstage performance shots in the U.K. from Glow in the Dark Part I before it hit the U.S.

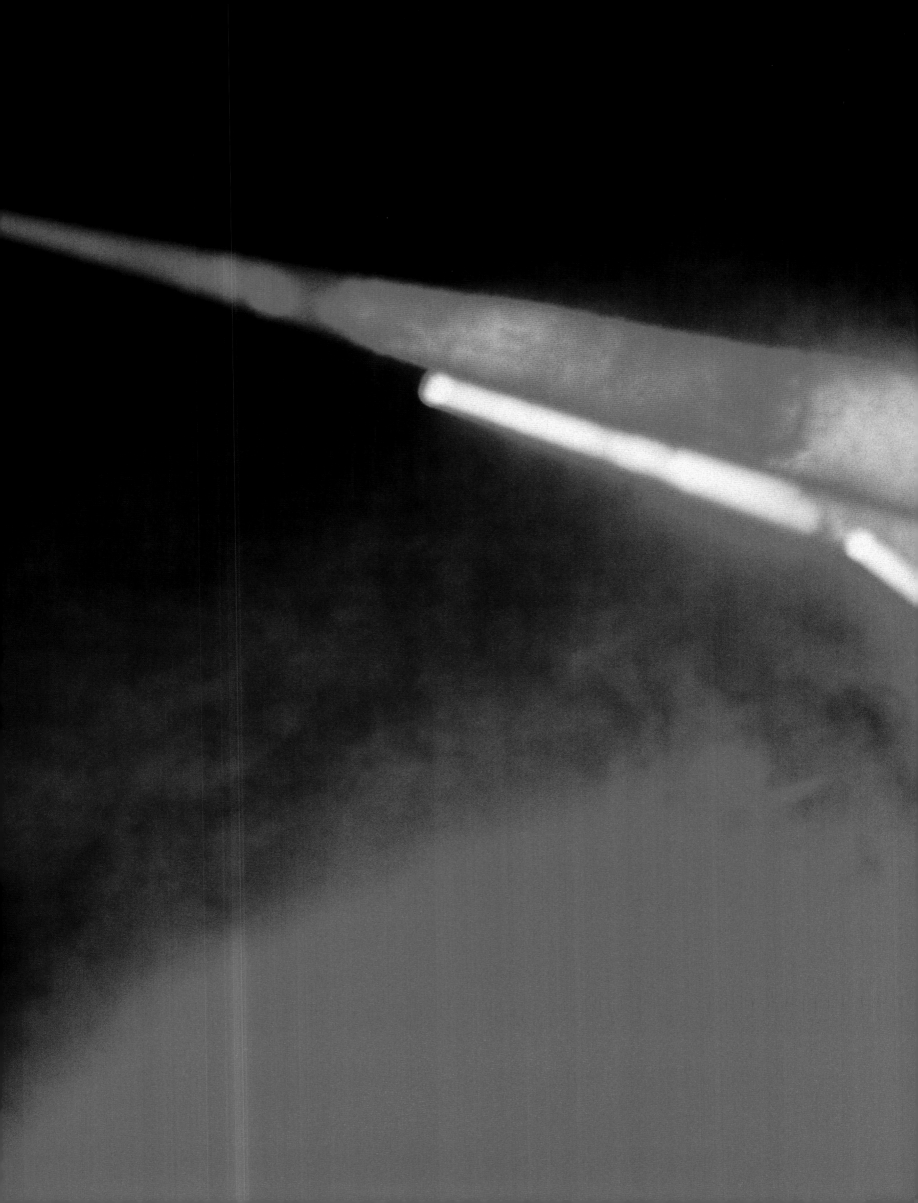

This is the robot woman Simon Henwood designed for this part of the tour. People were actually upset that we didn't have the robot girl once we came to the U.S. Simon's style is more *Metropolis*, more vintage-y; mine is more mod sixties, Kubrick-meets-manga.

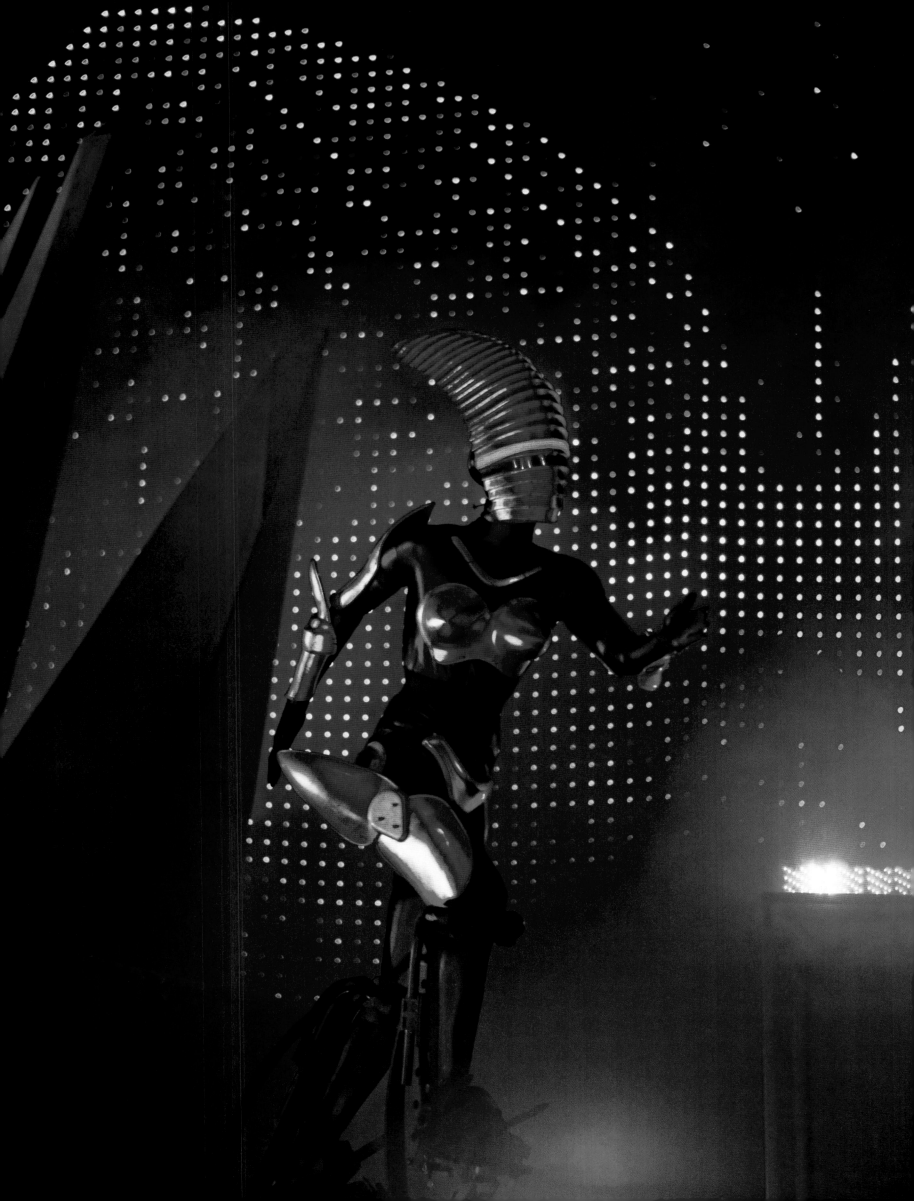

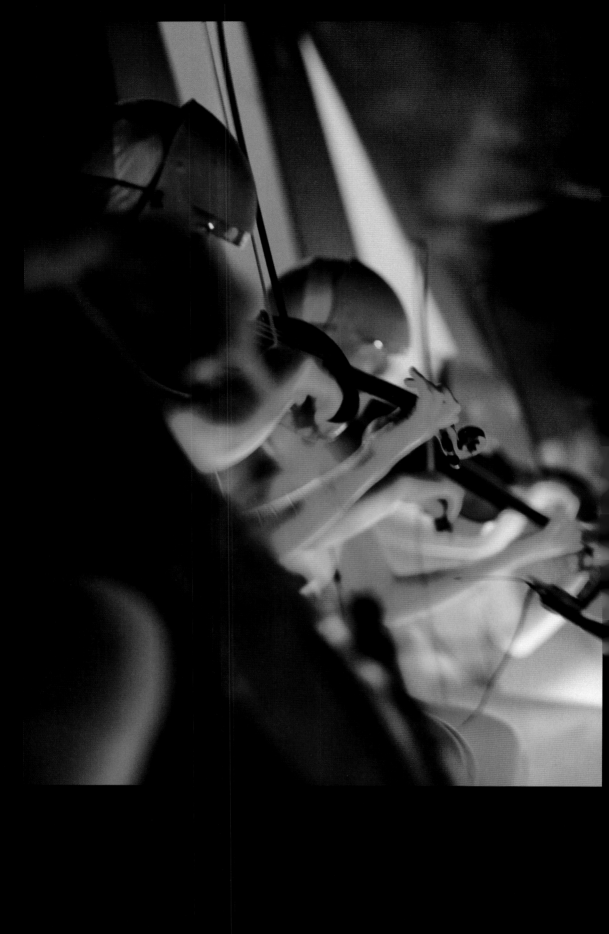

This is me, Don Crawley (my manager), IBN Jasper (one of my stylists), and Consequence unwinding after a show at a public bowling alley in the U.K. I hit a turkey (three strikes in a row). My score is next to the _K_.

This is you working out at the Sydney Opera House?

Yeah, and this had to be a few days after the Grammys, being that I still had my head shaved. It says "MAMA" in the back.

What's life like on the road at this point, three months in?

It's hard...what I was dealing with. At this point, I had just lost my mom a few months before.

While you were on tour?

At the very beginning of the tour.

FOLLOWING SPREADS Images from Glow in the Dark Part I in Australia.

43

The moon is full.

The wolf is out.

He makes his way through the jungle.

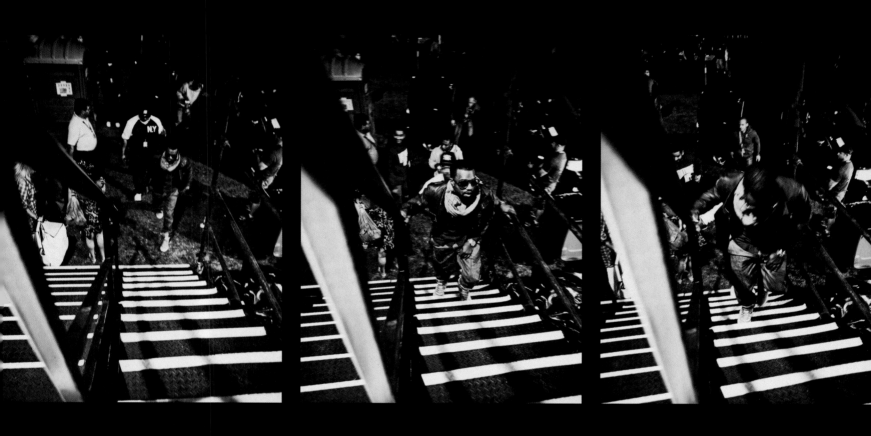

He spots his prey.

Steady, steady...

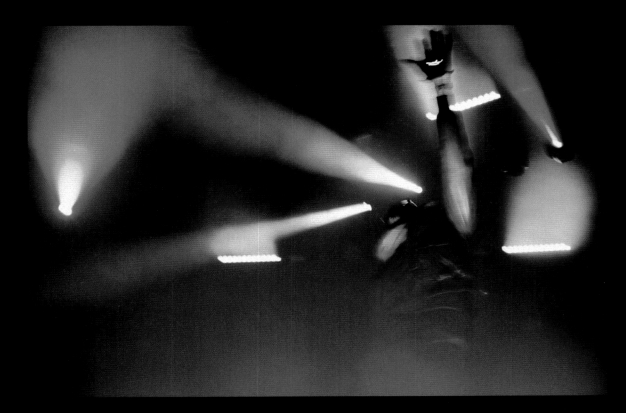

Attack!

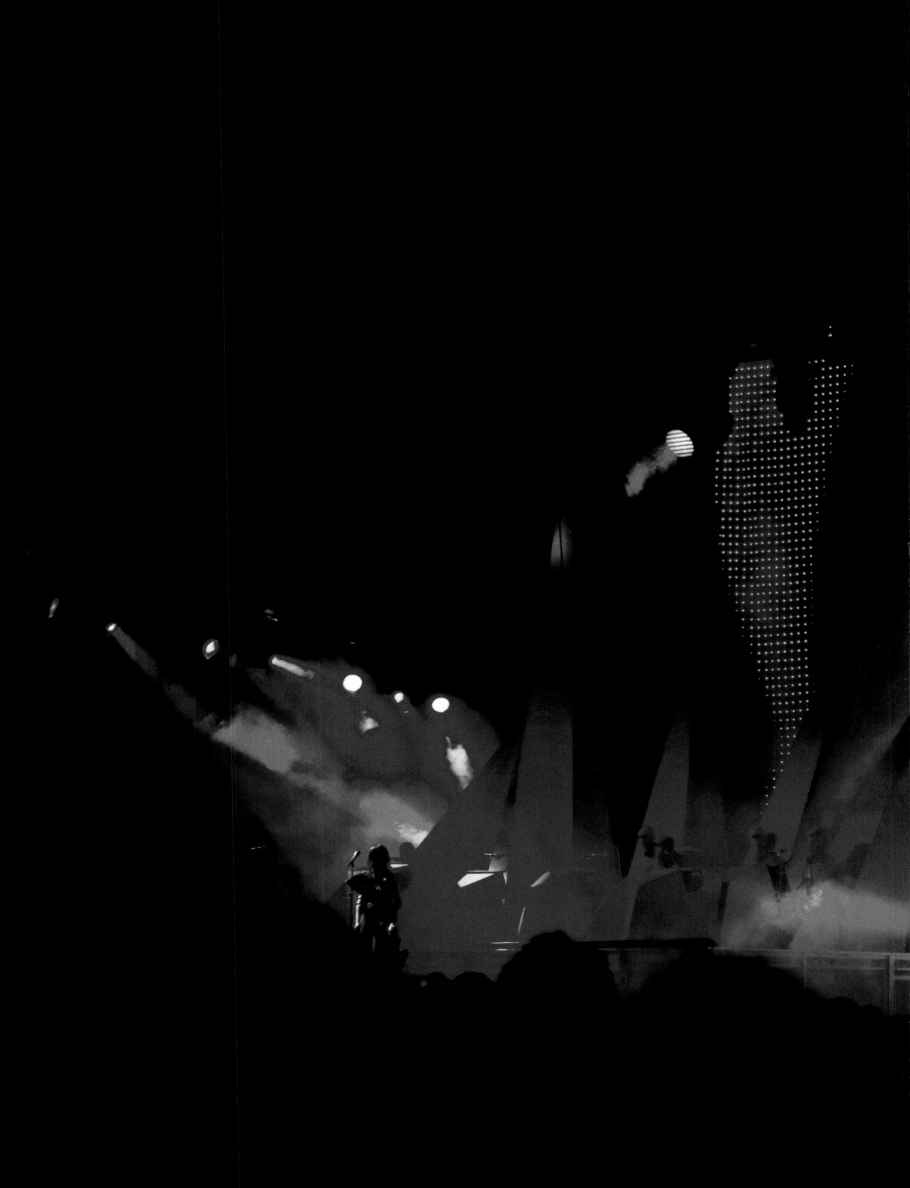

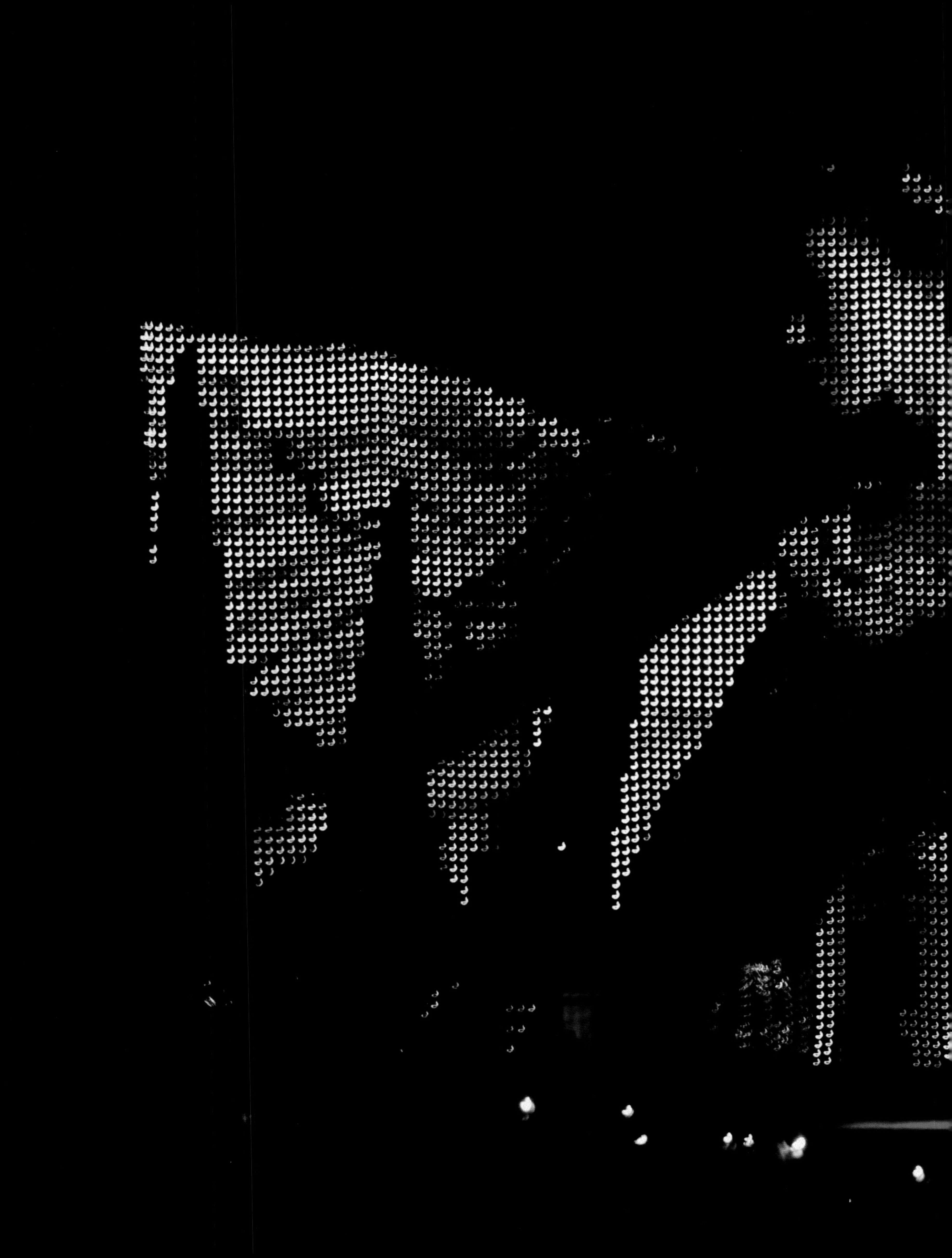

This is during "Hey Mama," when, after the crazy light show, we go down to this one simple lighting look and you can start to see the angel behind me. Some nights, it would be very emotional and I would be crying while I performed it.

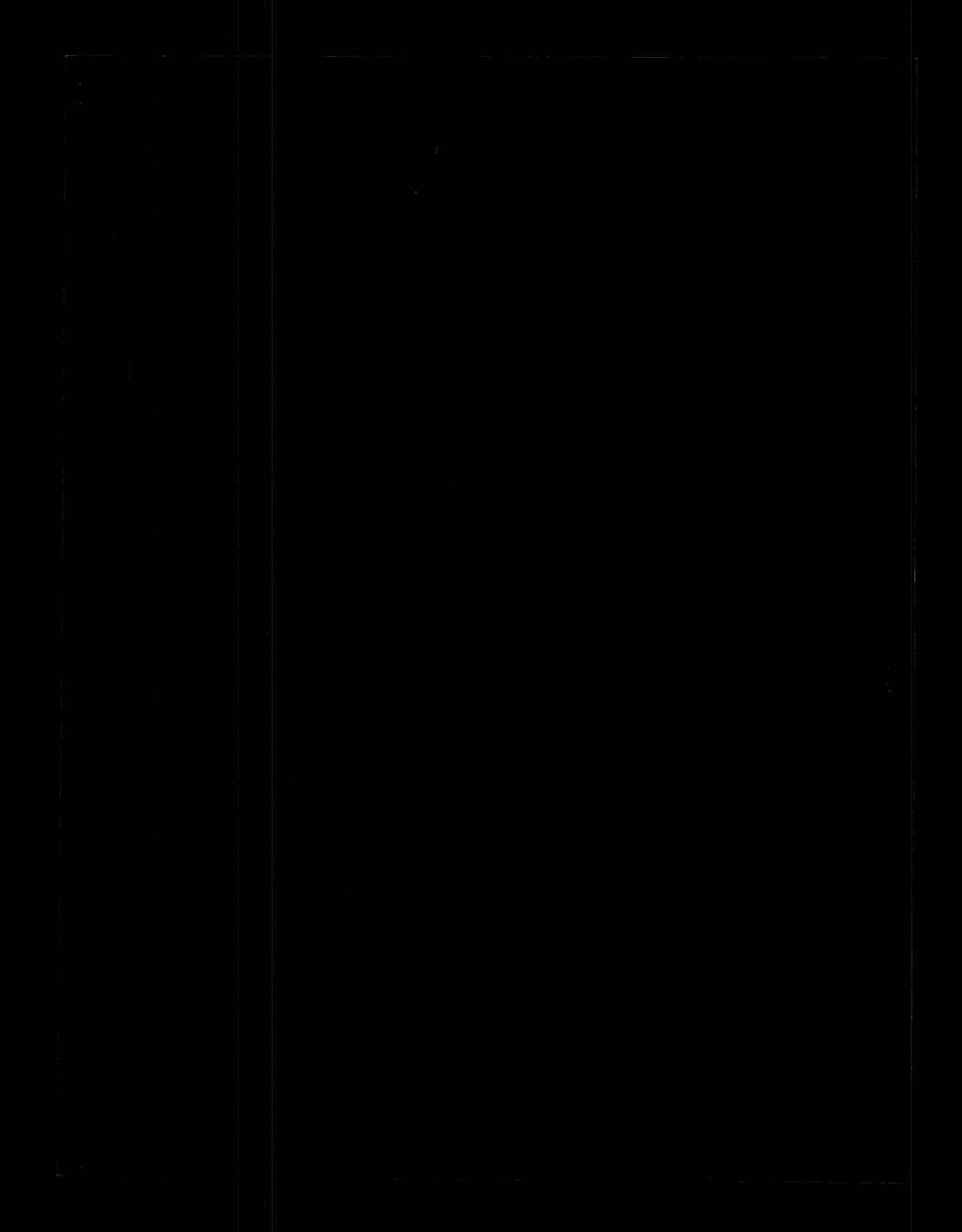

We're at the end of this leg of the Glow in the Dark tour, and I had full plans of bringing this version of the show to the States. But who knew that, after going to the Paris fashion shows, I would be so inspired that I would completely throw out all my previous ideas and start from scratch with a new tour that was starting up in less than two months in America?

GLOW IN THE DARK

COMPLETE REDESIGN

When you decided to redo the tour, you said you had sixty days from the time you got back from the Paris fashion shows. What was going through your head? In Australia, did you know you were going to do that? Or was it once you left Australia?

Actually, in Australia we had already started working on the new one. I was going to start from scratch, because we had to clean it up, make it more dramatic, more conceptual. We had to make it follow more of a story. We had to break it down to one simple idea to communicate. That was the hardest thing—to make it simple.

I think you had the idea of being lost, crash-landed on a planet. You had a lot of different characters; there was going to be a whole crew of people. Then we talked a lot about making that set really barren and dramatic. And talked about it being more theatrical than about the concert lighting and trying to simplify it—trying to pull some of the busy-ness out of it and letting it be more like a ballet, the lighting just really strong and simple and graphic. Also coming up with three basic acts. But I didn't really know what the story was. When you guys went off, you honed in on what the three acts of the story were. I don't know what the process of writing that story was.

I'd be in the studio, bouncing ideas, trying to figure out how these songs connected. Getting that *2001* [*A Space Odyssey*] kind of inspiration of the one character, J.A.N.E., being the spaceship, talking back. At first, the spaceship was going to be a guy, then we got to the "Gold Digger" thing, where she was going to turn into a hologram. Then it was, "Oh, we need to make her a girl, so this point works." It's weird; I was watching *The Office* today, and they give backstory on different characters out of the blue, and I wonder when they write this stuff. Like Stanley, the black dude who works in the office, said, "I won't apologize for anyone I don't feel like I'm right for. I told my ex-wife that, I told my current wife that, and I'm going to tell my next wife that." [Laughs.] This show has been going for four years; did they just write in that he had an ex-wife for that joke, and now they have to make everything work to it? Or do they have this basic information about each character? How far back do they go? Like that. We figured out that the guy is going to end up being a girl, just so that can work, halfway into writing the story.

Who did you write the story with?

I don't know if you know the singer Esthero, from Canada. She was in the studio, and she was the voice of J.A.N.E., and I bounced ideas off my friends, then also you. [Laughs.] "My

friends...and also you." My friends completely zoned out as we worked on the music. We had two different movies playing at one time on one screen. We'd just play them constantly, make this music.

When you were remixing the whole thing?

Yeah, because we went in and reorchestrated the entire album to sound like one piece of music. Whereas music usually sounds like, "Oh, that's from this album, and this is from that album."

You had to bring people in? Is that what my brother worked with you on? That sounds expensive.

What, working with all those different people?

Well, yeah.

I guess relatively expensive, like everyone charged thousands of dollars to work with me.

[Laughs.] I mean, to re-record orchestras, to re-record three records' worth of music.

I got my composers from Europe to redo some of the orchestra stuff. We wrote it in advance, and certain stuff we needed new strings on; certain stuff we already had files that worked together. I worked with three different producers—your brother [Spike's brother, Sam Spiegel, a.k.a. DJ Squeak E. Clean], Mike Dean, and Jeff Bhasker—and we stayed in the studio every day, reorganizing the songs, extending songs. Because what happens usually is you have your DJ tracks, and you sit with a band, and the band kind of figures out how to extend it. And all you're working with from the studio is that original track. I was, like, "No, I need to break open this original track and just use this drum sound; maybe just use this high hat right here, this sample, and run with this." Because I didn't want my music to sound like everything was a drummer with electric guitar over it. I wanted to have its specific sound.

How did you choose the tracks?

The ones that told a story, plus songs that I thought were good performance songs—songs that I want to hear every night. It was great to have that practice run with these songs, with the first tour. This is like the reshoot, and you're going, "No, we don't need this character now" and edit.

So you threw out the entire thing, started over. Did you make the date? Or did you end up having to postpone the tour—

We just barely made the date. It was a big issue. We didn't push it at all.

So you went and remixed the entire set.

I worked with three producers—Jeff Bhasker, Mike Dean, and Sam something. [Laughter.]

DJ Squeak E. Clean. Sam Spiegel [Spike's brother].

I worked with Squeak E. Clean, and he actually did do some really dope parts and helped a lot with the sonics. I went to the Daft Punk show. Every song was just knocking so well. If you go to a hip-hop show, sometimes they just have completely different amounts of bass from this song to that song. Your front-of-house guy has the opportunity to change the sound, too. And it disturbs me to not be in control of certain elements. We ended up getting a better front-of-house guy, but one of the complaints when we were on tour is that the sound wasn't that good. And the dude, he would talk to me and try to explain why it was someone else's fault. We got somebody else after the tour was over, but every tour you grow. You get a better this guy, a better that guy.

You have a sound guy for the next tour?

We have a really great lighting guy, really great stage designers, lighting programmers, a really great MD [Music Director], great producers working on redoing the music, really great graphics people. But U2 didn't happen overnight. What's so incredible is for this tour to be compared to some U2 shit, and it's only my second major tour to keep on taking information. I went and saw Coldplay at Abbey Road, and I saw their lighting guy, and I fired my lighting guy the next day in the middle of the tour. I was, like, "These guys are so much better." I guarantee you, whatever drawbacks for two shows or one show that there are, it's going to make so much difference. And sometimes, when you're fighting a war, you have to just retreat for a couple of days.

You fired the lighting—was that lighting guy on this tour?

Hell to the no. Got rid of the newer lighting guy. I got a newer, newer lighting guy. I got a newer lighting guy after that and then a newer, newer lighting guy after that.

So the Coldplay guy was good until you fired him?

I didn't fire him. He went out with the Killers, then I found a really, really dope guy who I still work with.

And did the guy who designed the lights for this, design the Daft Punk lights, too?

Yeah. But he didn't do the European run.

So you're saying Squeak E. Clean helped with the sonics?

Yeah. We've got to go to another page, though. [Laughter.]

TOP Mixing board with set list for the tour. MIDDLE Mixing in the studio. BOTTOM, FROM LEFT TO RIGHT Me and Pharrell at the board.

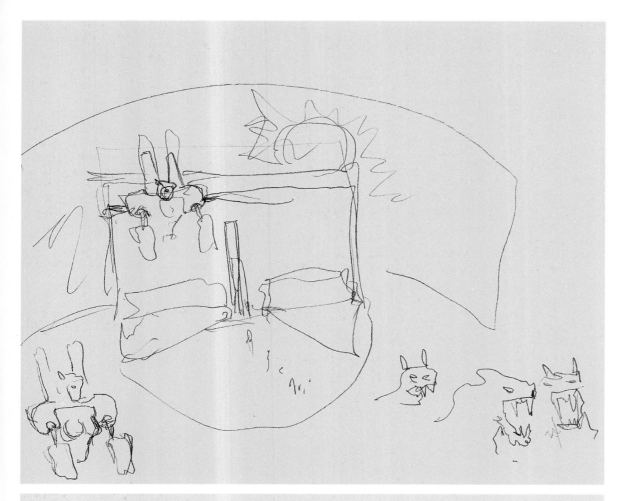

Is this the set?

This is one of the drawings when I alone was coming up with this and not working with any directors or going by their offices, asking for any advice.

After you abandoned trying to get help from everybody else?

Yeah, actually I was vibing out with this dude Spike Jonze on this part right here. He was, like, "Man, why don't you make a big giant car?" I was, like, "I don't know. I just want to make a robot." I was into a specific style of robot, and the idea is that the robot is inanimate—or you think it is—and, at some moment, it lifts his head, and that's what the Jim Henson people are going to do, because I wanted this massive thing onstage. I was going to have it try to attack me—me against this robot on this abandoned planet. We eventually went from that idea to making it me and this spaceship, and making the robot—the mechanical thing—be on my side. Some of these sketches are just ideas. At one point, I had this idea that it was like a giant wall of robots, which would've been really fucking cool-looking. Once we decided to finally get this simple idea where I crash-land on the planet—well, me and my spaceship—I wanted to have all these characters and monsters come out. But we could only afford one, so these are some of the preliminary sketches for the monsters. Then we worked with the Jim Henson team. We spent countless time sketching. I remember giving them references of an Aston Martin and a shark for the face. I was very specific about how I wanted my monster to look. Everything represented my style, and this is *my* style of monster. The Jim Henson people did an incredible job, and it was really great to work with them.**

Why did you want to get Henson? What did they bring to it?

Just a nostalgic, very authentic feel—and to be able to say that you work with them. I was going to Henson Studios meeting with Daft Punk, anyway, because they have an office in the Henson Studios. I would stop by the Creature Shop.

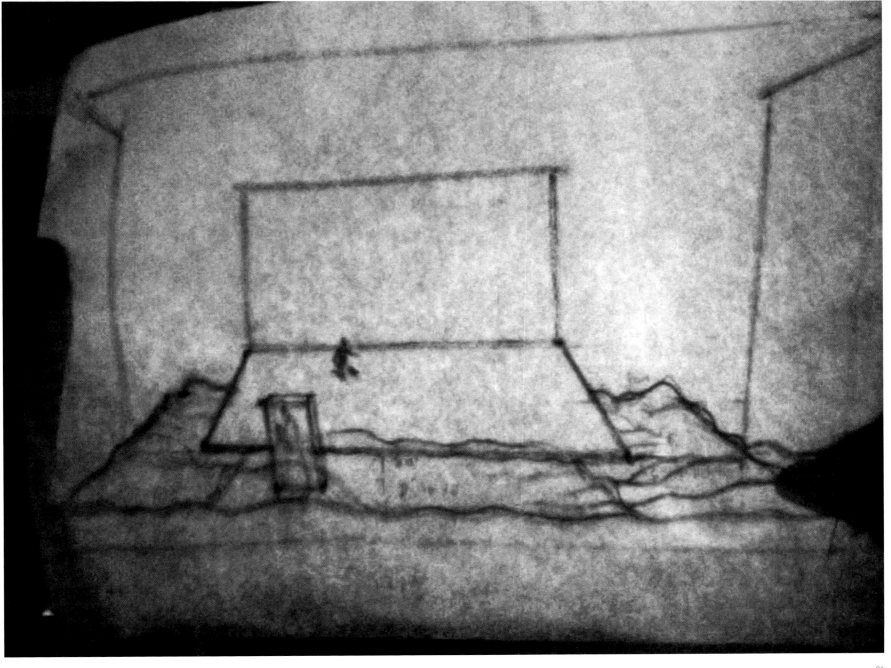

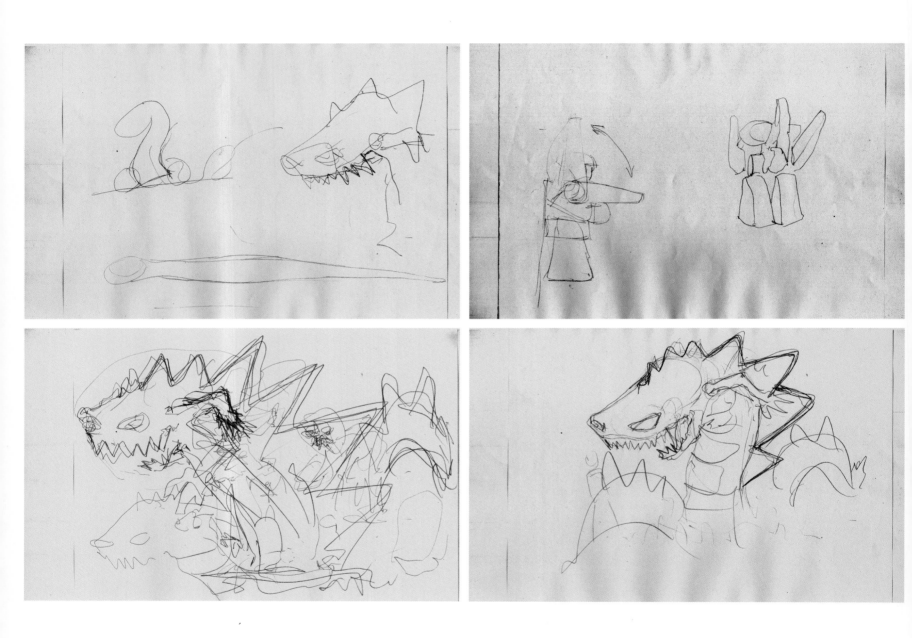

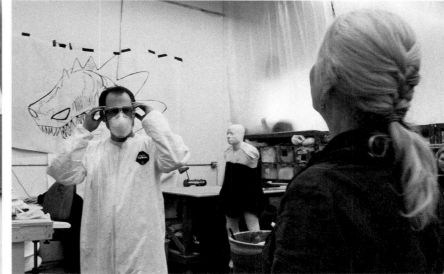

THIS SPREAD Creation of the monster at the Jim Henson Studios.

Everything represented my style. This is *my* style of monster — a shark feel like the Aston Martin DB9 or the SLR McLaren.

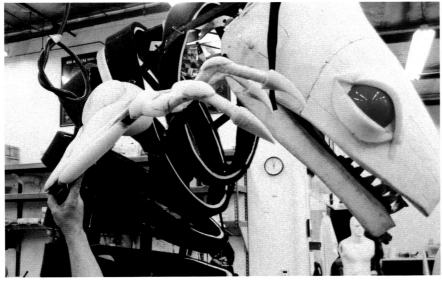

These are some preliminary sketches I did for the "Gold Digger" girls. You can see I was all about showing skin to win. I'm into sex. I don't know about other people, but to me it feels really good, and I like it.

I think anybody who's spent more than five minutes with you definitely knows you're into sex. You talk about it a lot. I think if you talk about it a lot, you must think about it even more.

No, I don't.

Every time you talk about it you're thinking about it?

I basically talk about what I think about, if I feel comfortable around people. If not, then I'm, like, "I'm meeting with Barack; no, it's not a good time to talk about sex."

Who else do you not talk about sex with?

That's about it. Barack is like a living version of Jesus. Everybody's, like, "Man, Jesus, I don't know how to talk about sex around you, because the fact that you didn't even come from sex—you know, Immaculate Conception or whatever—and before that, the rib was produced, and the woman was produced by a rib..."

Skin, you like it.

Skin to win. These are some of the outfits we were thinking of for the "Gold Digger" girls. I was thinking of some real sci-fi shit off the old school, like *Barbarella*—to have the juxtaposition of this mechanical spaceship then everything else be very natural—from the shape of the stage to the monster, to their outfits. I wanted to have these women with ridiculous bodies—sexy, all gold-painted—shot to look like holograms projected on the screen behind me while I performed the song. What happens in that scene is, I'm talking to J.A.N.E. and—you'll like this one, it'll be completely unexpected from me—the spaceship was supposed to take off and we were supposed to make it home. Then there wasn't enough power so we crashed back on the planet. I'm, like, "J.A.N.E., I can't believe this. I haven't been home in so long. I haven't had a woman in so long. I need some pussy." I said that, and the audience was, like, "Oooh," and every night somebody would come up to me and say, "Man, you don't need to say 'need some pussy.' It's just so crass." I'm, like, "Fuck you." [Laughter.] I think this is really good—something Will Ferrell would say, and that's like my idol. He's like my living Jesus.

Will Ferrell and Barack Obama are your living Jesuses?

No, I didn't say Barack Obama. I look way up more to Will Ferrell than Barack Obama. [Laughter.]

But you said he was Jesus, too.

More people look up to Barack than Will Ferrell. I just personally look up to Will Ferrell.

So Will Ferrell's your Jesus? Can you talk about sex with Will Ferrell?

I think I would have a conversation, because my Jesus likes sex. My Jesus didn't die a virgin.

Wait, Jesus died a virgin?!

You didn't know that? That was the whole thing.

Is that for sure?

Yeah. I had this rap where I said: "You know what's a crazy thing?/Some girls will make you wait longer than A. C. Green/Passion of the Christ, 33-year-old virgin/That's disrespectful, baby don't encourage him/I like them brown, yellow, Puerto Rican or Persian/Dashiki kimono or a turban/I dress so white but my swag's so urban/Trying my luck/I hit her with a text like 'baby you up?'/question mark and she respond 'Yes S-I-R'/That's 'yes sir.' " [Laughter.]

ABOVE Hype Williams shot and directed the video of the girls to look like holograms.

This is me working on some of Rihanna's outfits. The final thing was really cool because I went to the fencing store and grabbed some different shield armor and had it painted black and put it on her body suit. We made three outfits for her, and these are some of my preliminary sketches of the boots and different outfits.

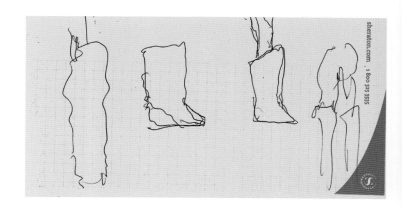

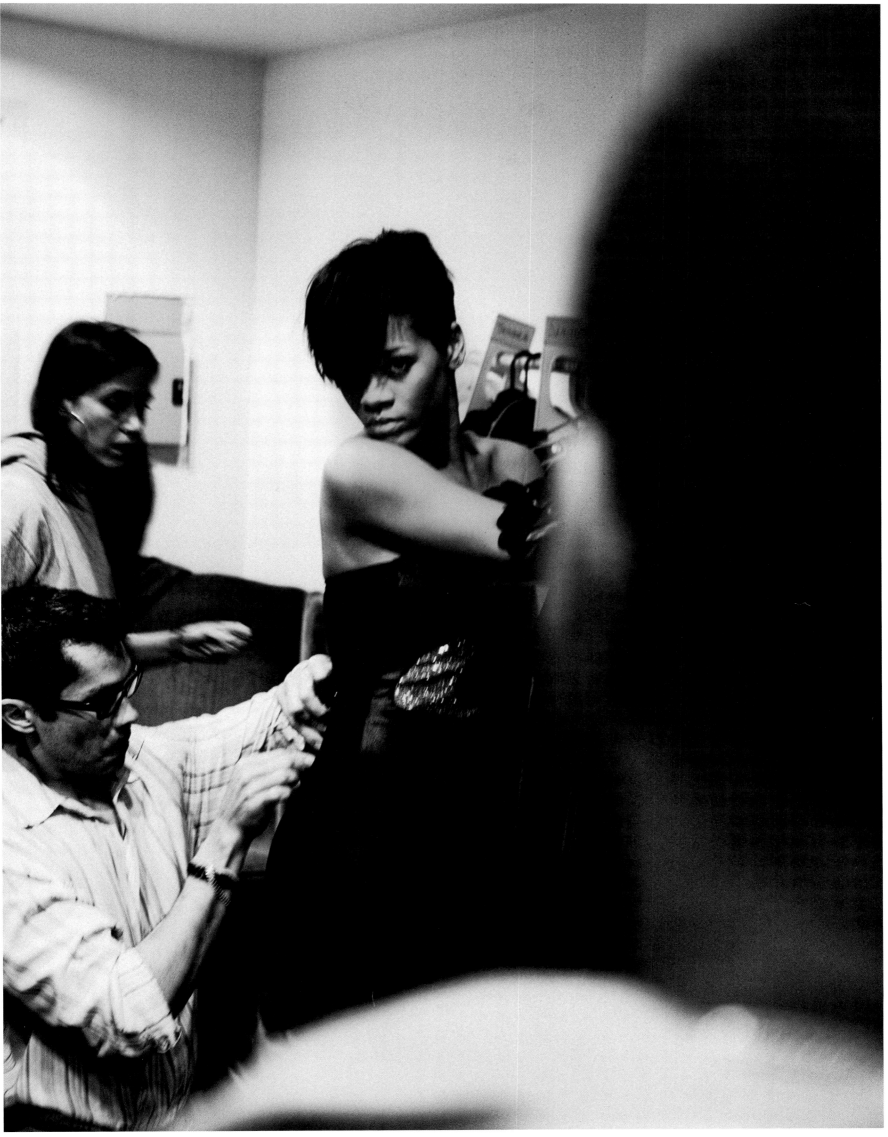

BELOW I created this gown-and-hood piece for Rihanna out of rubber and tulle. I also designed outfits for my backup singer, Joi Starr [left]. I was really inspired by Grace Jones and that tough, futuristic look.

But she wasn't in your set. You designed her clothes for her set.

I designed clothes for her set because everything is my set on this tour. We sat down every night and challenged ourselves. Halfway into the tour, N.E.R.D. got a bigger screen, and Lupe—they changed their lights. Everyone became better touring acts. They're, like, "We have to step this up," because, by the time my set hit, it was so mind-blowing.

This is the jacket I did for her.

Why did you do outfits for her?

Originally, she had some outfits done by—I won't say what brand, because I don't want to knock it—but I just felt like, with her being her, her thing could have been even more dramatic than it was. The reason I put her on the tour is to throw her in the lion's den with credible artists, like me, Lupe, and Pharrell—take this pop princess and throw her right in the middle of it. I really felt like, as a true artist, she was authentic and that the problem was people around her trying to give her what pop was today. There was a time when pop was really dope, like Madonna and Michael Jackson, Phil Collins, and Peter Gabriel—that was pop. Now they're trying to make pop be— I'm not going to name the names of what's pop, but it would be some shit where you wouldn't want to do a video for these people, you know?

I used to email pictures of these maquettes to my friends to let them know how I was about to kill the scene. Then I started blogging these pics to get everyone as excited as I was.

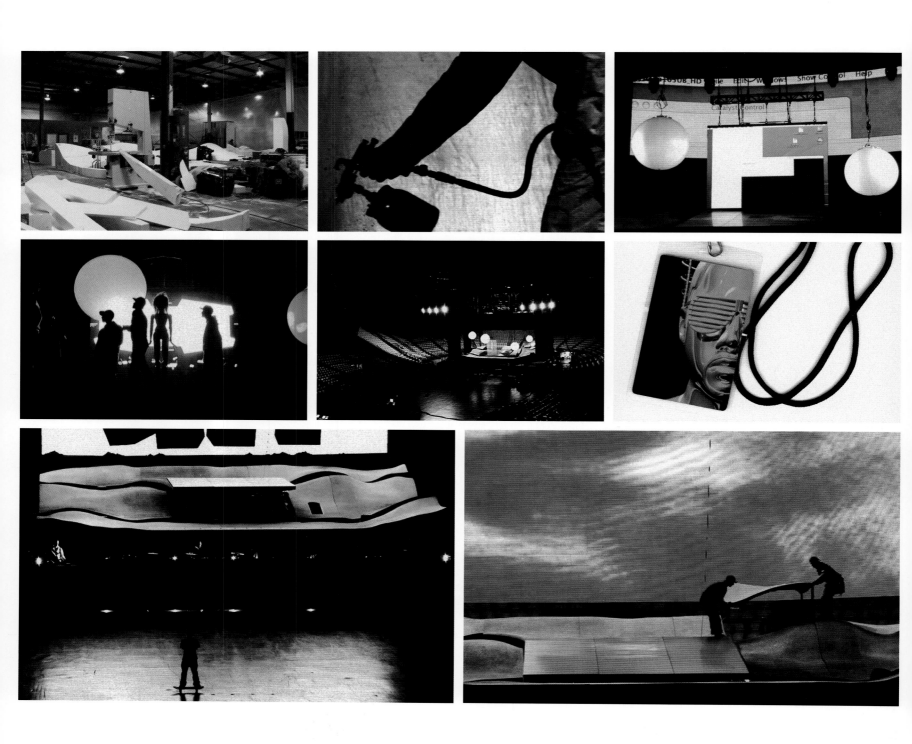

THIS PAGE The actual construction of the stage from the molding, welding, test runs, and rehearsals. OPPOSITE Working on my outfit with some of my stylists.

When I was a child, and watched sci-fi films, I used to take my mom's bed sheets—she had this one quilt that was blue on one side and white on the other, and I would take it and flip it to the white side and put pillows under it to recreate the planets in the movies. I would set all my characters up on it and be one of the characters. If you really think about it, that's exactly what my stage was. When things are truly inspired and meant to be, and they just flow through you in some way, the true inspiration for that was that childhood that came through me, where I was, like, "I have to tour, and I don't want to!" But if I'm going to do it, then I'm going to dress up like a spaceman. When I was in kindergarten, they did these tests and they had me draw, and I was, like, "Can I draw a football player?" And they were like, "No, just draw a regular guy." I was, like, "Okay, I'm going to draw a regular guy, but I'm going to put a football player outfit on him." This was my response as a kindergartner. I'm mature now, but I'm still going to flip that bed sheet over and try to make a snow planet.

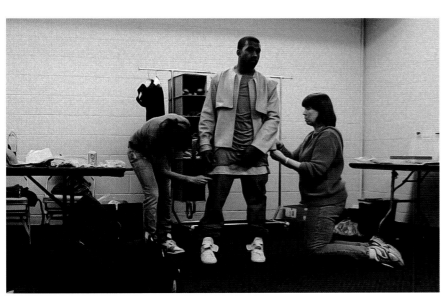

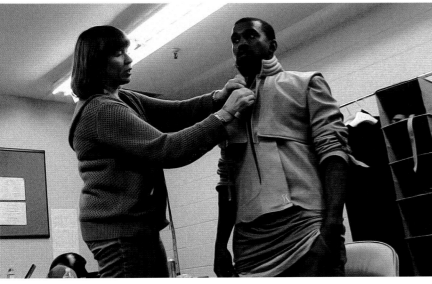

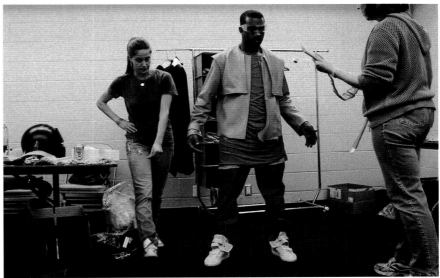

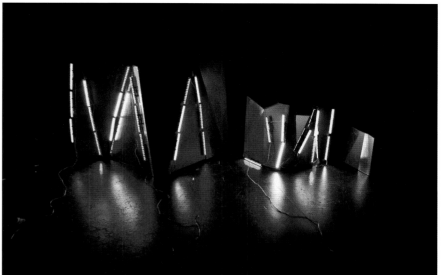

This is me working on Rihanna's actual stage. We designed it with these lights inside; as you see, it even looks cooler right there. This can run all types of rainbow lights. It was running lights and turning red and doing different things.

Didn't you say you ran out of lights—that you bought all the lights in New York?

Yeah, originally the lights were supposed to run all the way down, and we're, like, "Oh, we ran out of lights. Okay, just put them at the top. We're going for more of a snowcap feel." We put this thing together so quick, but I knew it would be more dramatic. We hadn't done New York, and she had got some reviews from different people where they said they didn't like it as much, and I knew about it. She was coming right after N.E.R.D., and I wanted her to really impact people. I want people to know that we brought her on this tour for a reason. So I went and just redid the set.

This was the second set?

This was the set. She had to go out on the New York show and perform on this set for the very first time cold. I had to talk her manager into it, because they wanted to use the old set. But I was, like, "You have to use this newer set. This is the Madison Square Garden show." And that's the first time people saw that set.

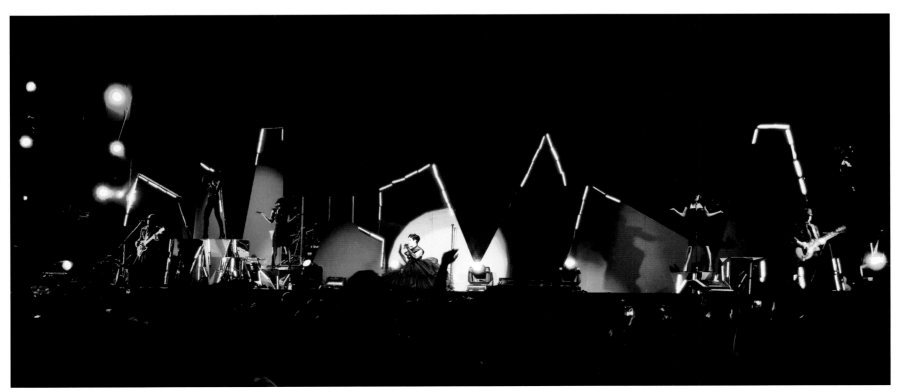

GLOW IN THE DARK

PART II

04.16.2008 — 08.07.2008

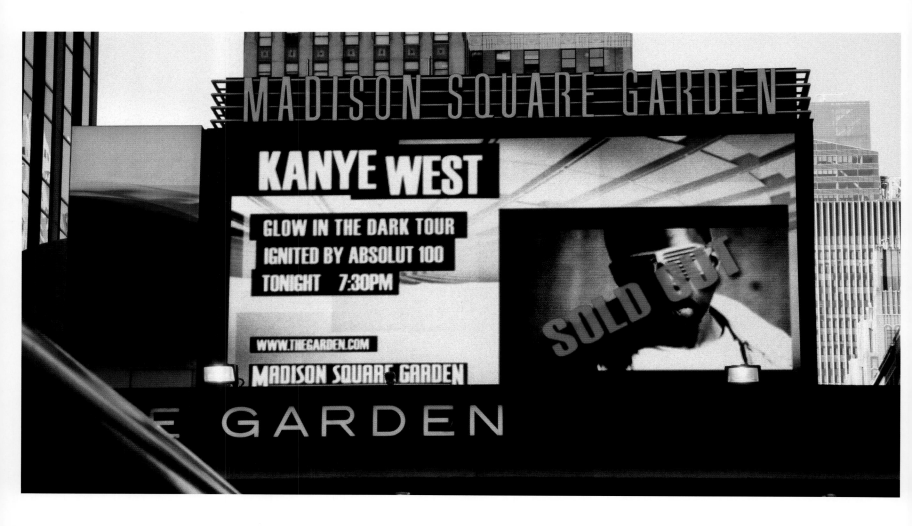

I initially toured North America from April (in Seattle) to September of 2008, then came back to certain cities because of demand, selling out huge arenas a second time around. I performed at Madison Square Garden in May, then again in August of 2008.

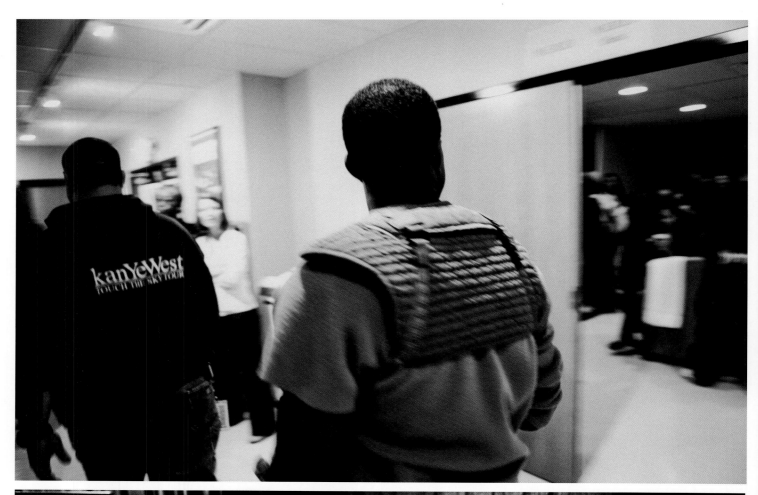

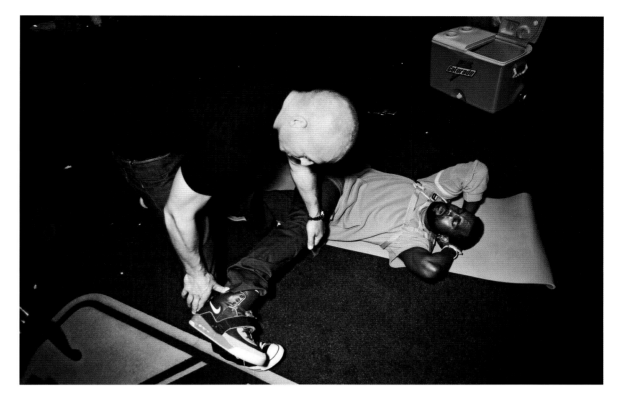

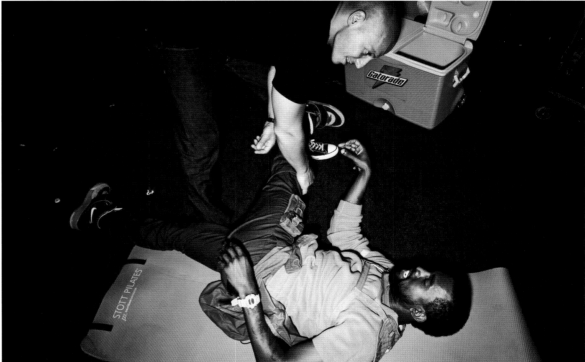

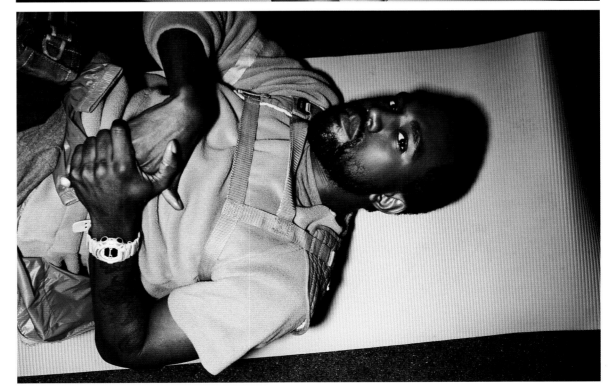

This is Lupe. He started off, and it was amazing because Lupe is such an ill, credible rapper. He's arguably a better rapper than me, and he's very stylish and has a lot of rock-star swag. This tour was all about blatant fucking icons—no joke. There really weren't opening acts. Everyone was a closing act on their own terms, and we just put them all together. It was a combination of everything, like if you went down to Fairfax right now—all those stores. This is the tour version of *Hypebeast*.

Then you get Pharrell, who's actually my personal idol and one of the most stylish people ever and one of the most innovative people in music ever—to have N.E.R.D. on tour—they used to just rock out. He didn't do any non-N.E.R.D. songs. He's just like N.E.R.D., period, and that's what we're doing. He'd bring people onstage; it'd have that type of energy. That's what they were doing.

Watching N.E.R.D. perform.

THIS PAGE Pharrell and Lupe backstage in Chicago.
OPPOSITE With Common backstage in Chicago.

Let's talk about backstage. You guys actually hang out?

Yeah, and everybody is skateboarding and stuff. A few people played basketball every day. It was like a field trip. It was the coolest shit, the coolest artists. It was me, Rihanna, N.E.R.D., Lupe, and every place we went, it's like Common pops up, some superstar would pop up, and we'd be playing ball or Connect Four or just watching games, going to the studio, recording new shit, rapping, people skating in the hallways.

THIS SPREAD With Rihanna and her dog backstage in Sacramento.

115

THIS SPREAD Various backstage shots in the U.S.

FOLLOWING SPREADS Glow in the Dark Part II onstage shots during my U.S. performances. This is how most people saw the tour.

sequences on the screen behind me as I performed my
show in order of my set list.

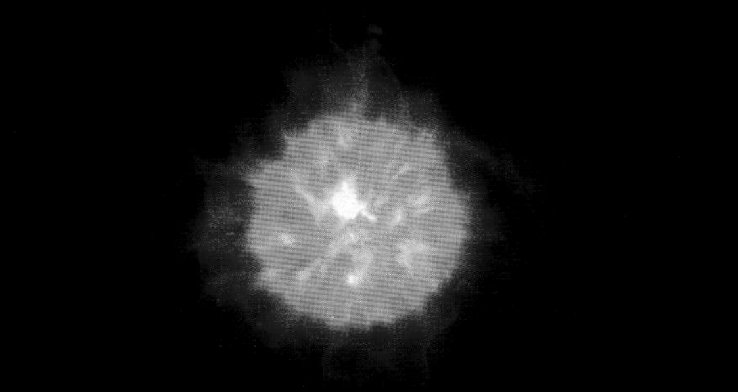

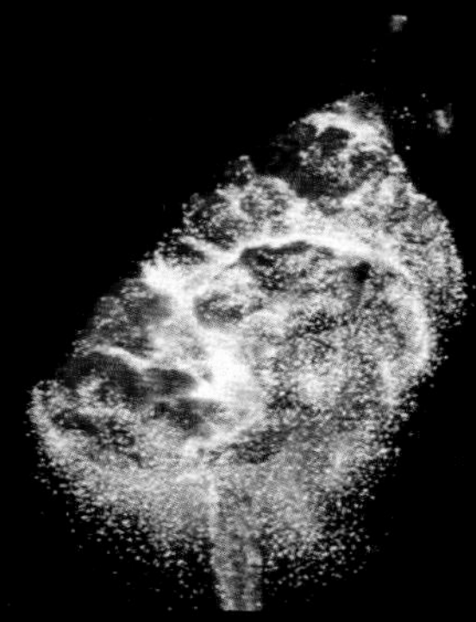

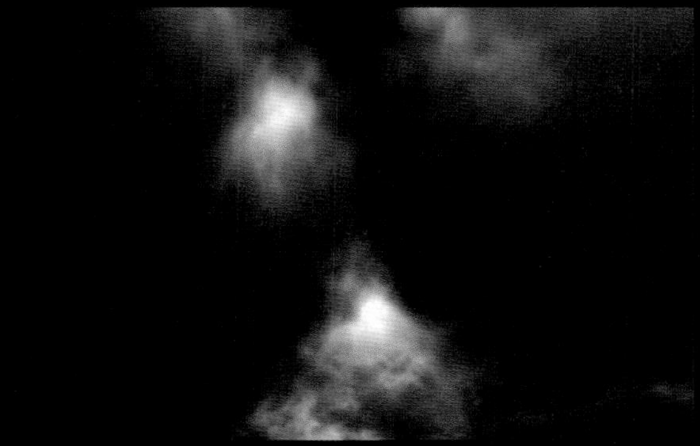

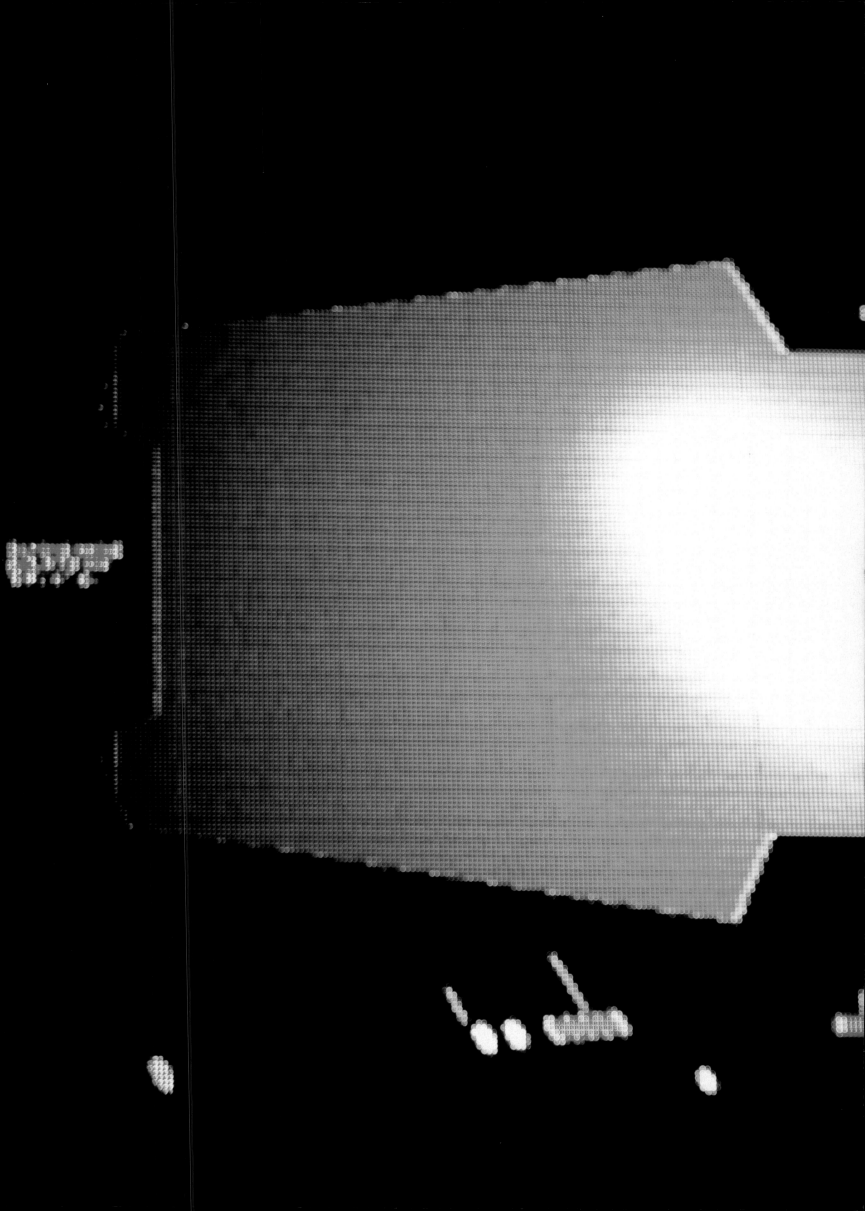

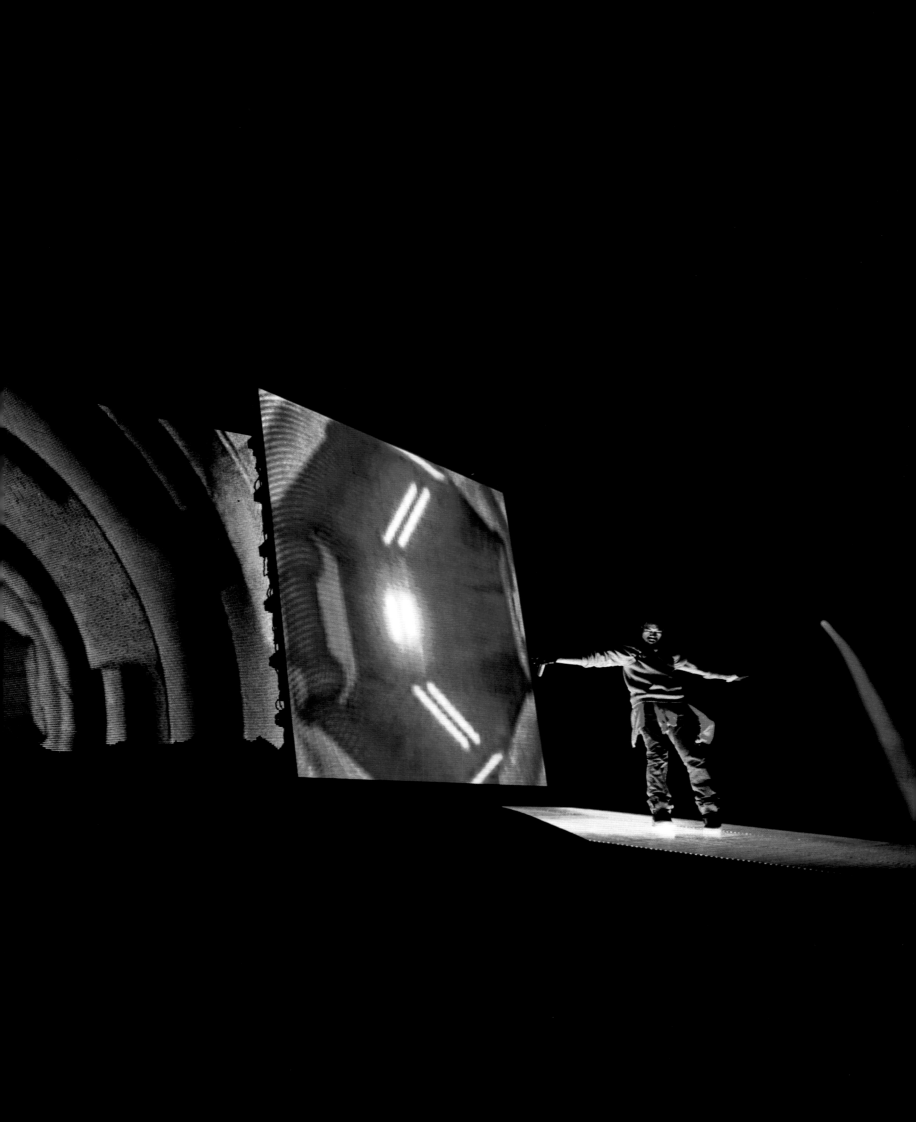

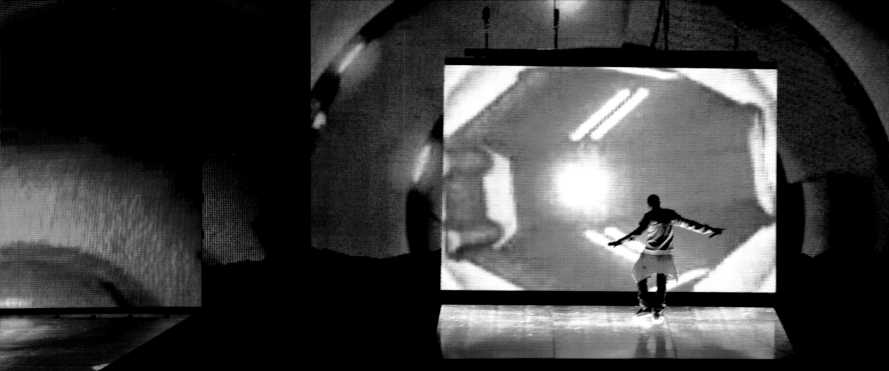

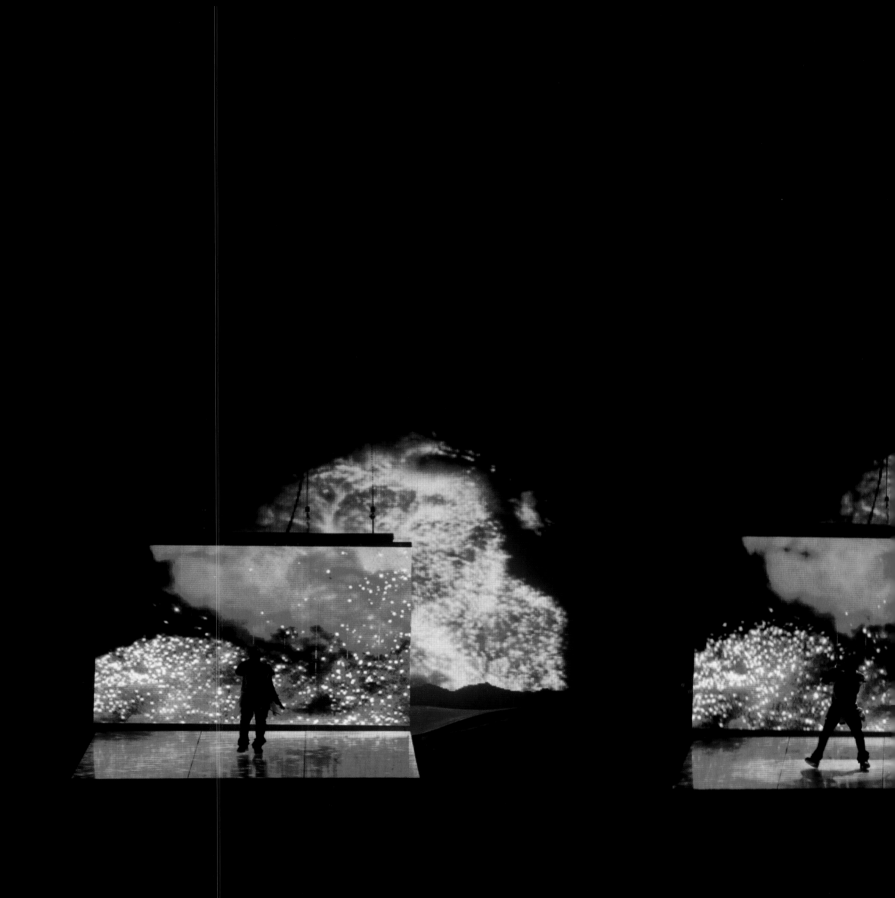

I love looking at this book because I get to see what people were seeing. Like this image—I was up there, thinking, this has to be really fucking cool to people.

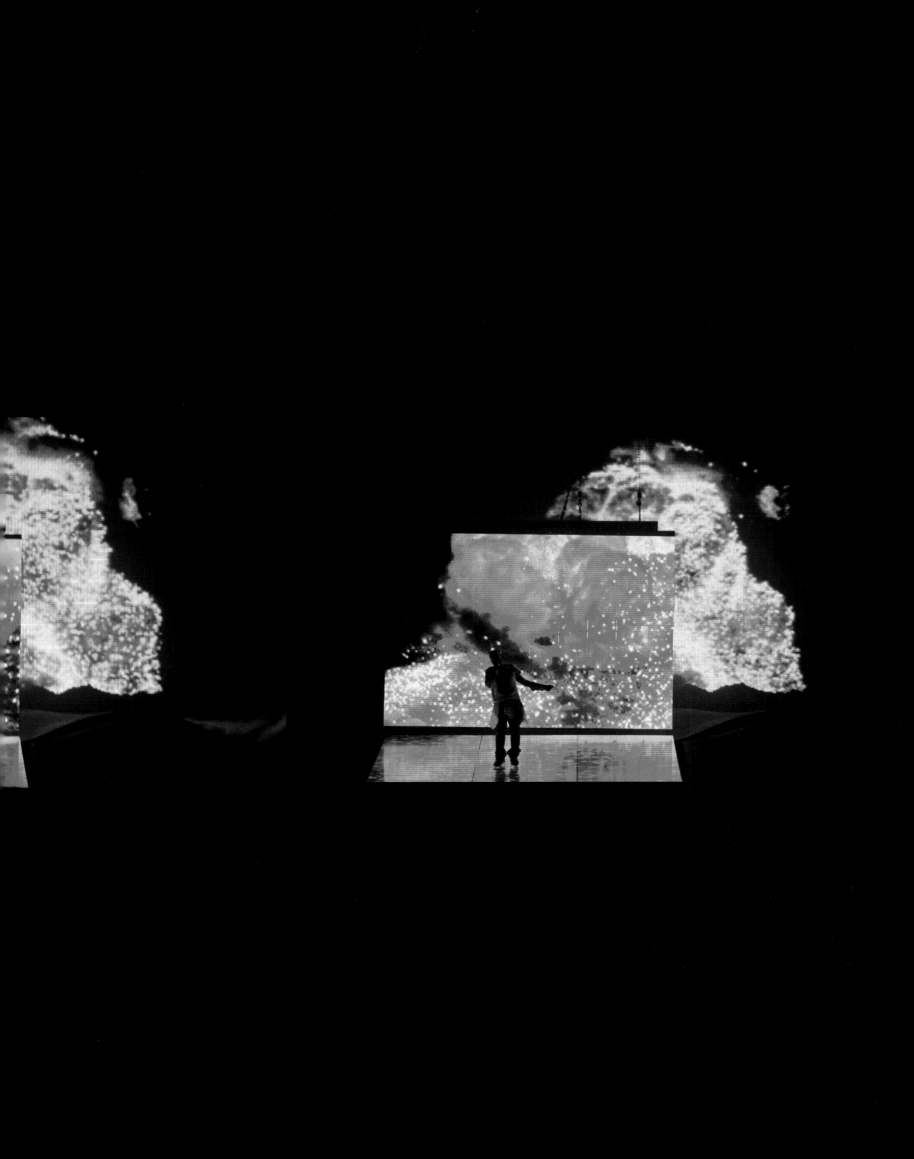

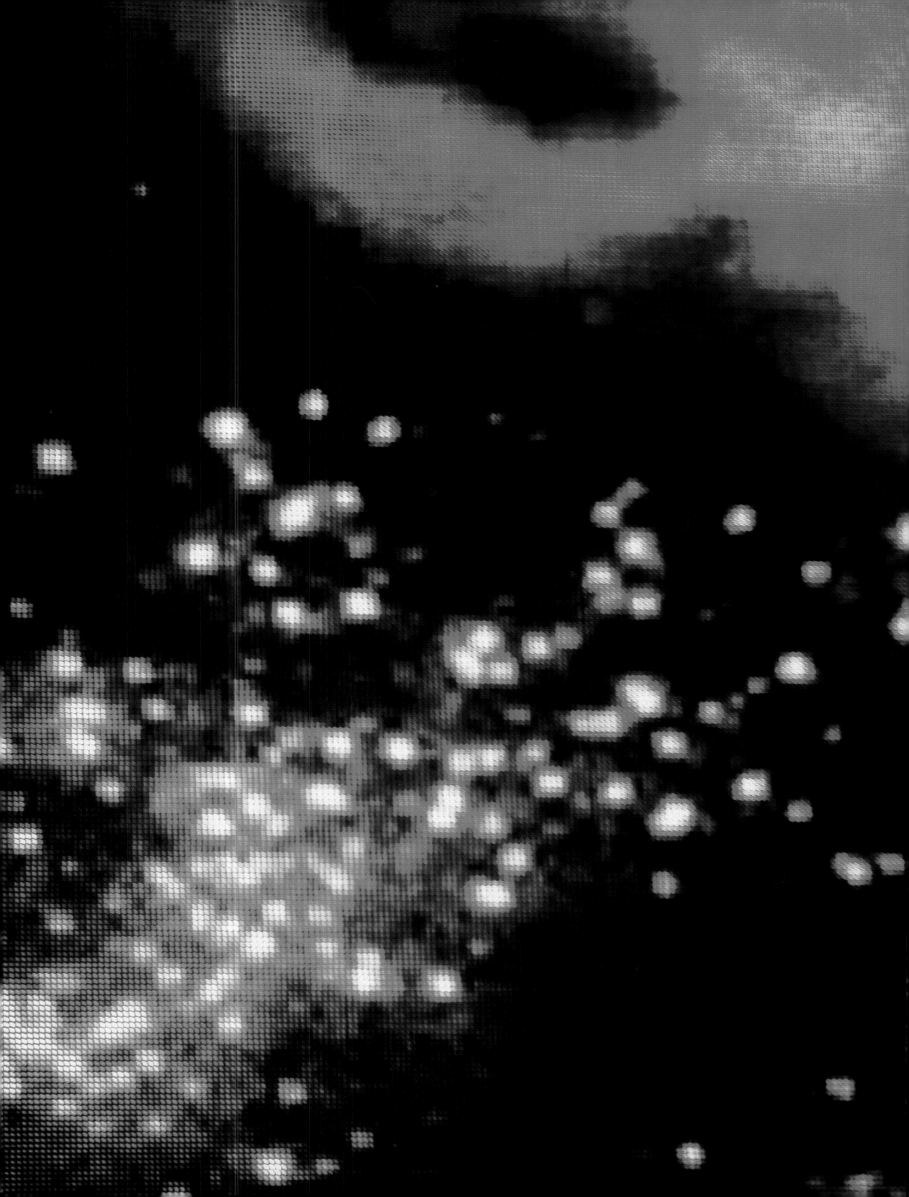

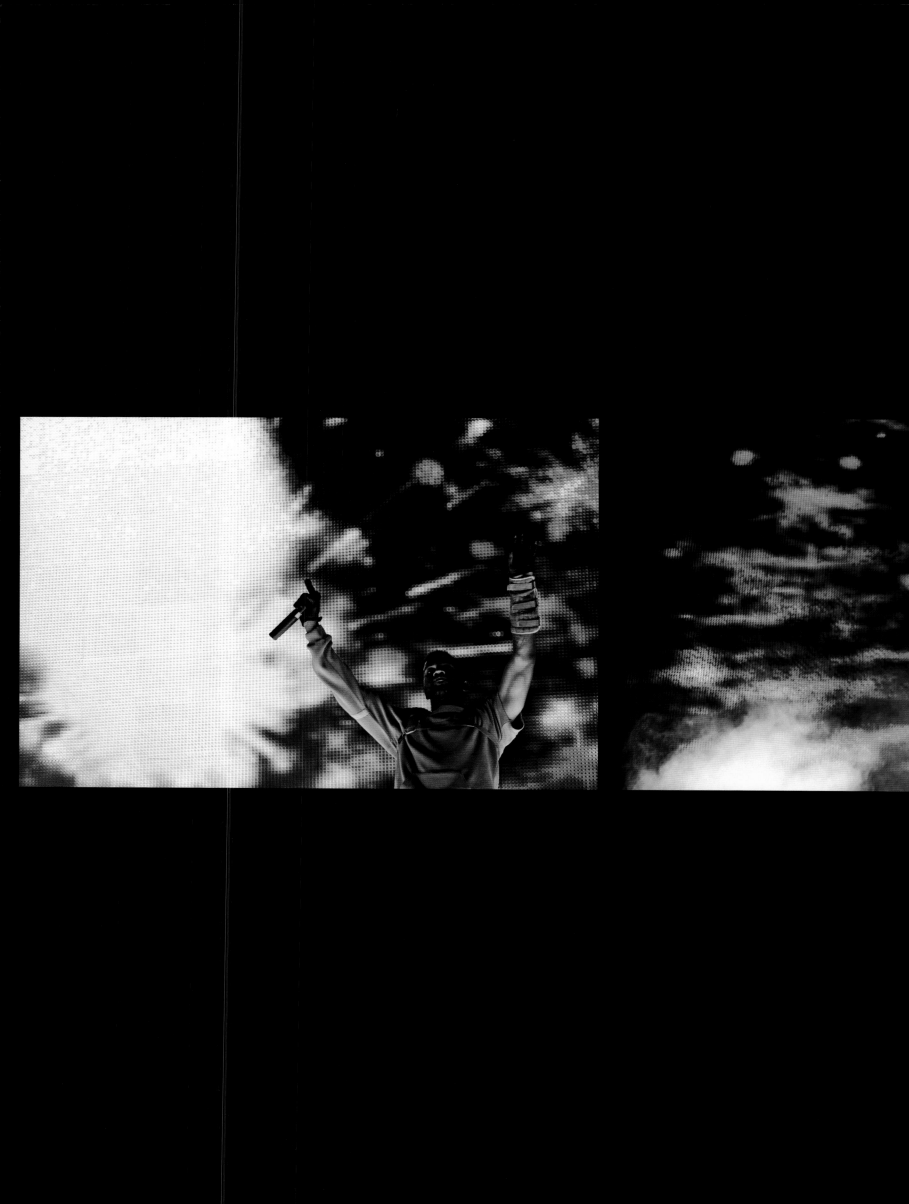

we had this really dope, spooky music and it was lit like a movie and the monster's moving. It's Jim Henson puppeteering.

It was the intro of "Can't Tell Me Nothing" and I'm like, "J.A.N.E., I know I'm not on this planet alone. I hear something, I feel something," and the monster starts making noises.

How many people controlled it?

Three or four.

What happened when it swallowed you?
How long were you in there for?

A minute, maybe two.

Were you still singing while you were in his stomach?

No, the monster was just making eating noises and shaking.

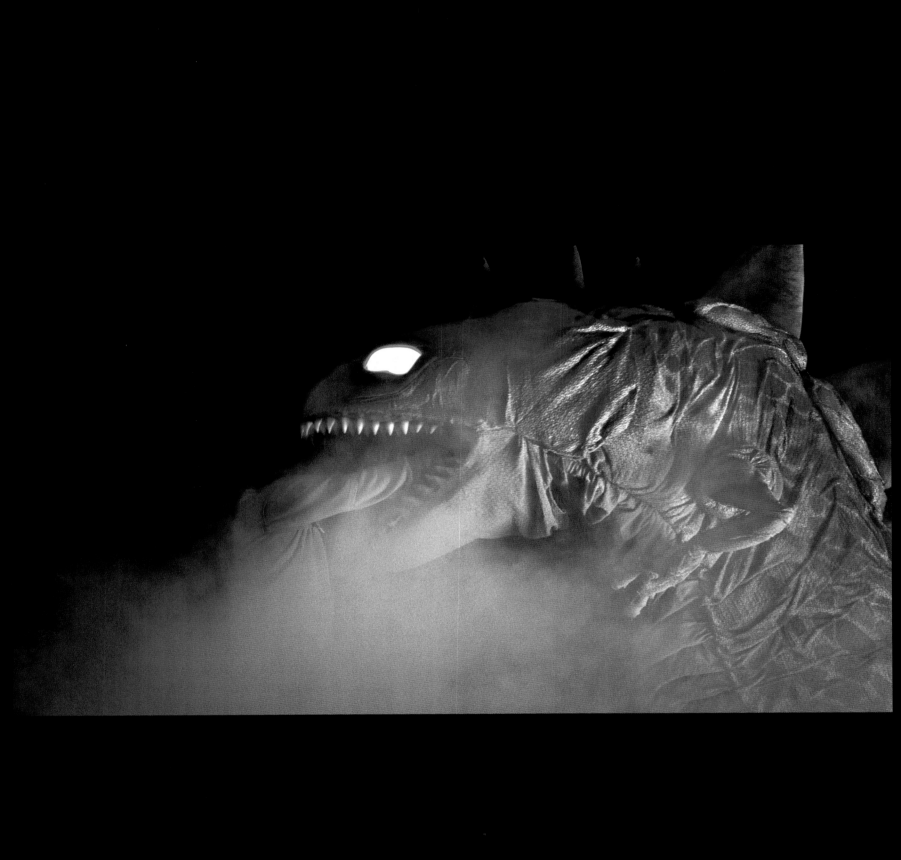

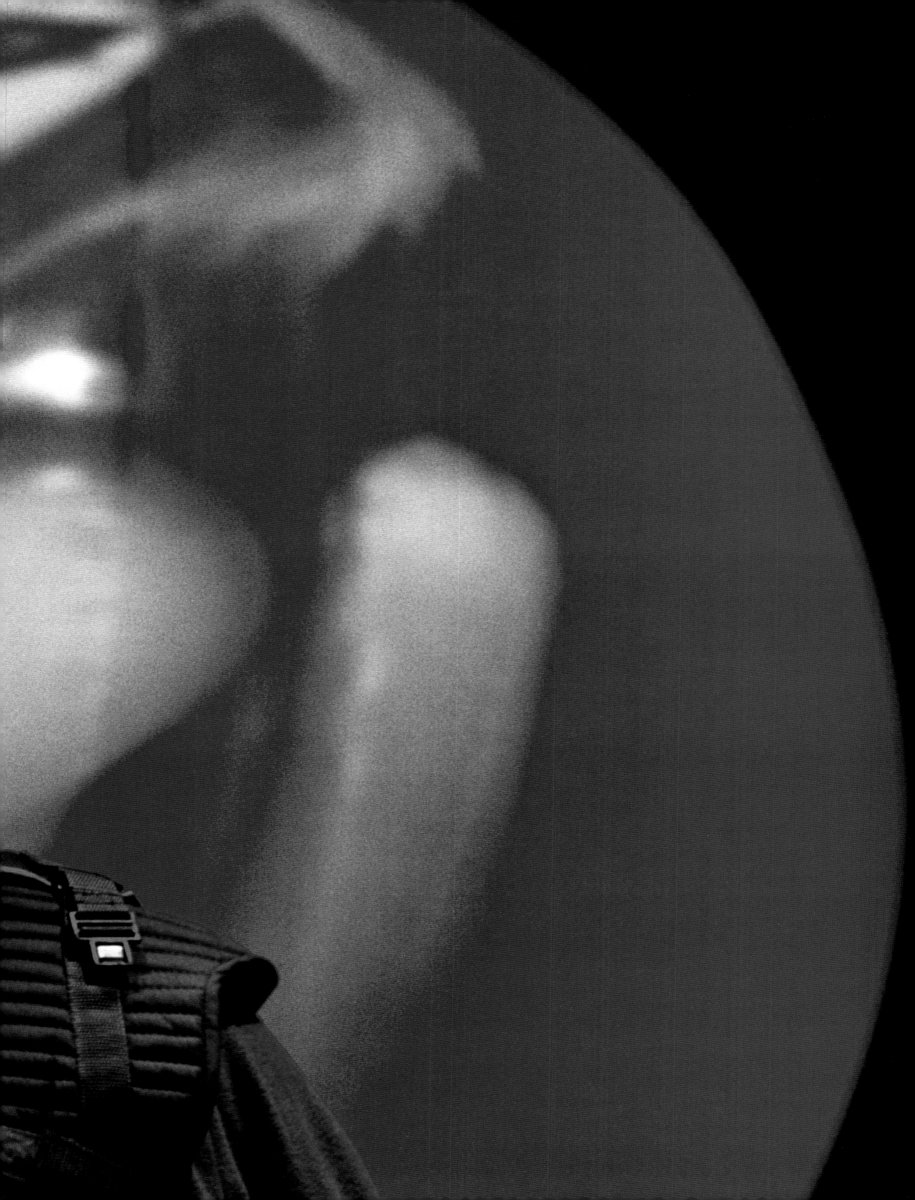

J.A.N.E. helps power up the spaceship but there's not enough power. She says, "Those shooting stars didn't have enough power. They're here today, gone tomorrow. We need something real. We need the brightest star in the universe."

And who would that be? [Laughter.]

"We need you, Kanye."

No way.

Performing the Journey hit "Don't Stop Believing"
as my grand finale. The eighties song became popular
again after being used in the "Sopranos" season finale.

Everything's a sunrise, sunset, a million colors on the screen. I was sticking to the point of doing biblical skies to have that juxtaposition between nature and electronics.

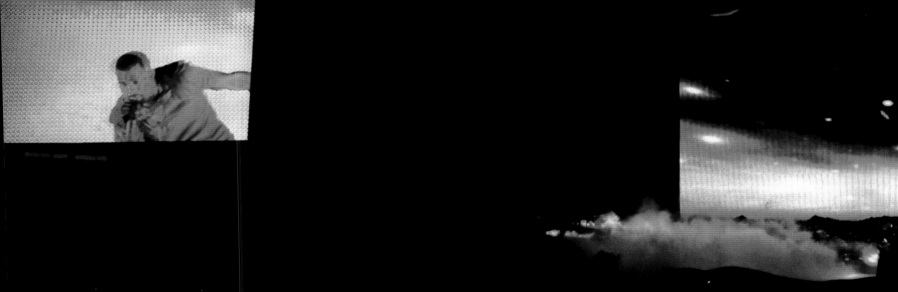

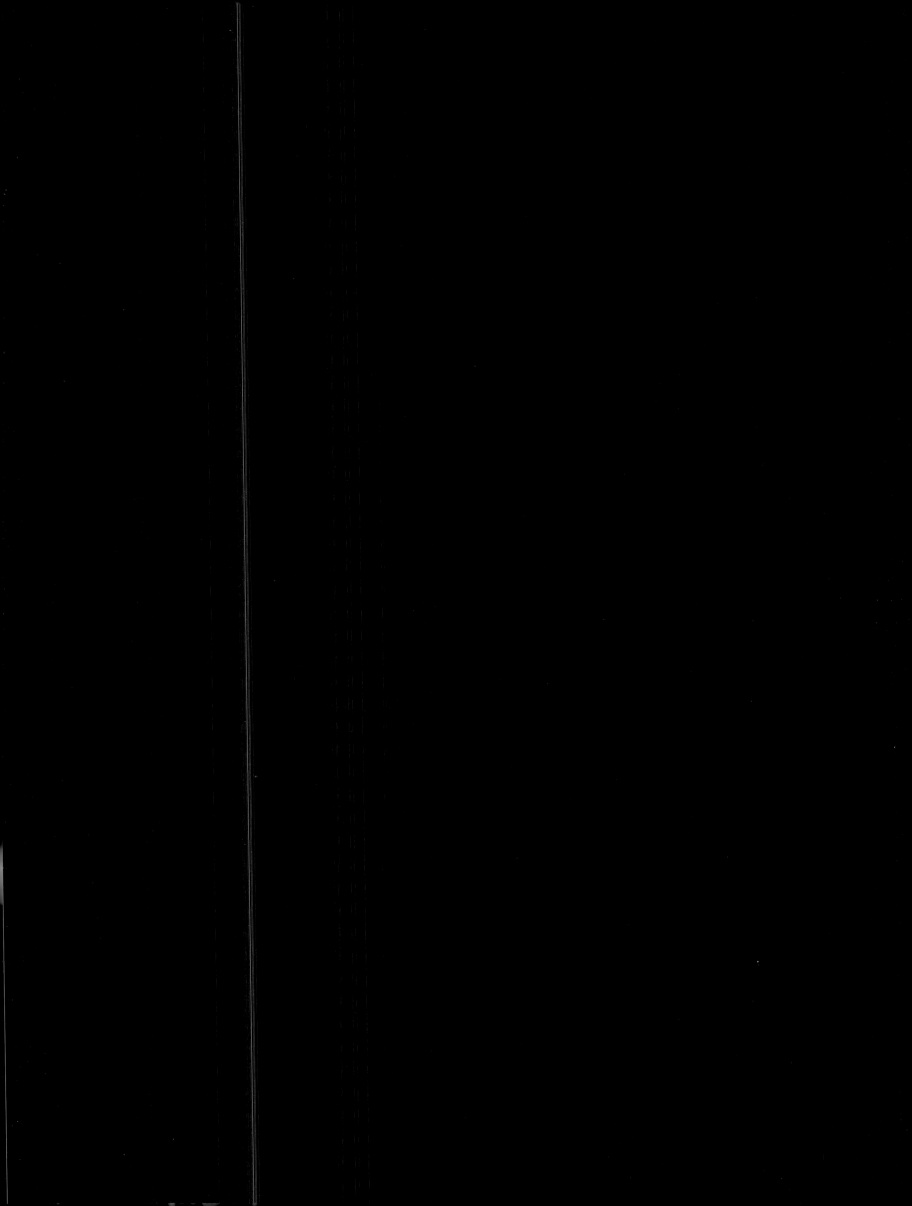

A special performance at Madison Square Garden with Jay-Z of "Jockin' Jay-Z," a single from his new album out that year.

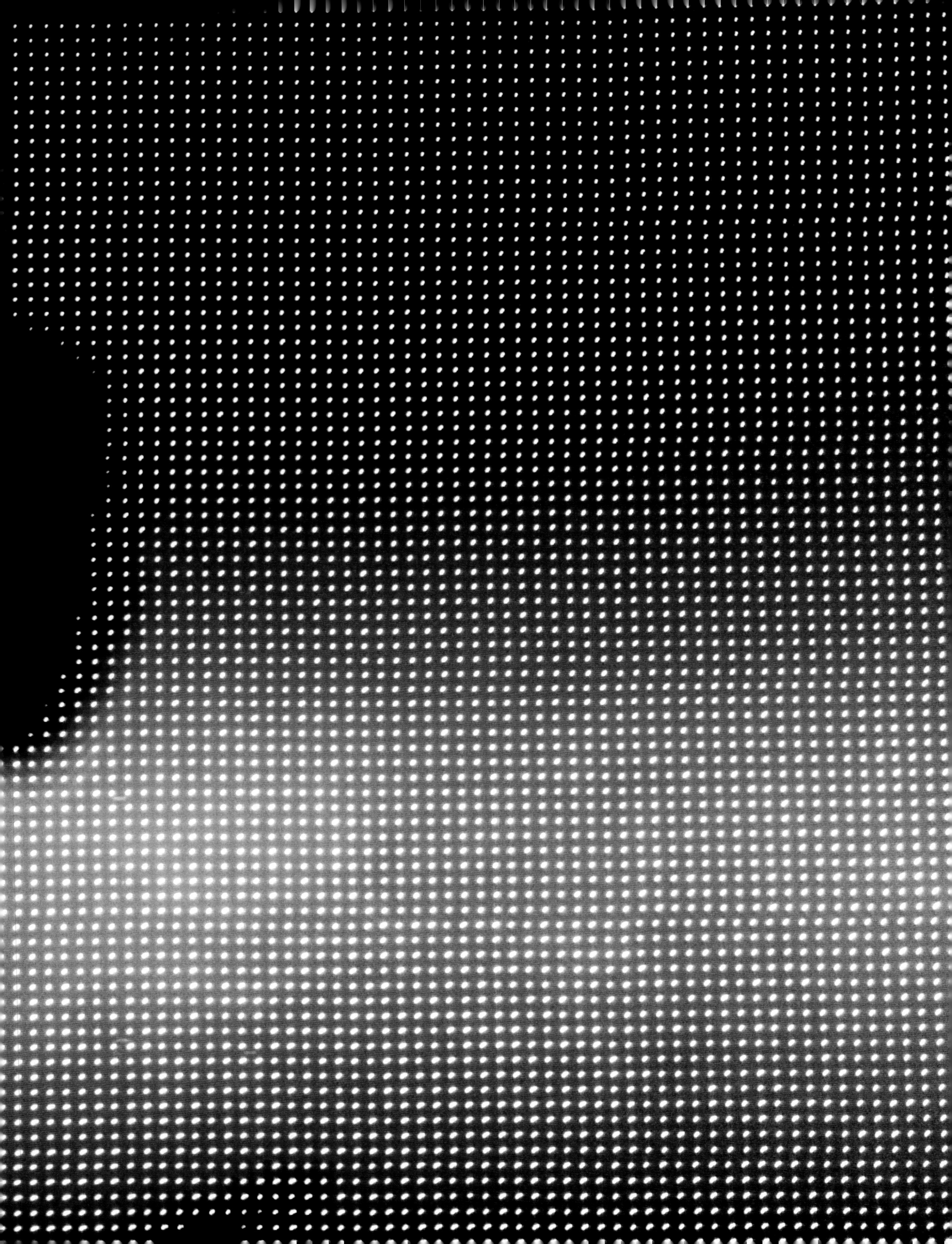

THIS PAGE, CLOCKWISE Me and Jay-Z; Me and Ludacris.
OPPOSITE PAGE, CLOCKWISE Scarlett Johansson and
John Legend; Questlove; Ray West, my father; Will.i.am;
L.A. Reid; Q-Tip.

CASIO G-SHOCK
25TH ANNIVERSARY PARTY

In the midst of the tour, I have some other stuff I do—like this G-Shock party. I was in my straight madman, seventies-rock, don't-touch-my-hand-I-have-gloves-on mode. No one knew that we were going to have these naked alien dancers. I designed the set for this, too. I put this chair in the middle of the stage, and, for the whole first four songs, I performed the songs sitting down, and people were starting, at the end of the songs, to not clap anymore. And that became very funny to me. [Laughter.]

So you sat down for another one?

Eventually, the girls came out by the third or fourth song, and people were, like, "Oh, shit!"

Was this your dream come true, having naked alien chicks?

Yes, one of my dreams. That's what life is about—naked alien chicks.

Where do you find these girls?

Man, there are a lot of people who like to get naked. I don't know.

You seem to know a lot of them.

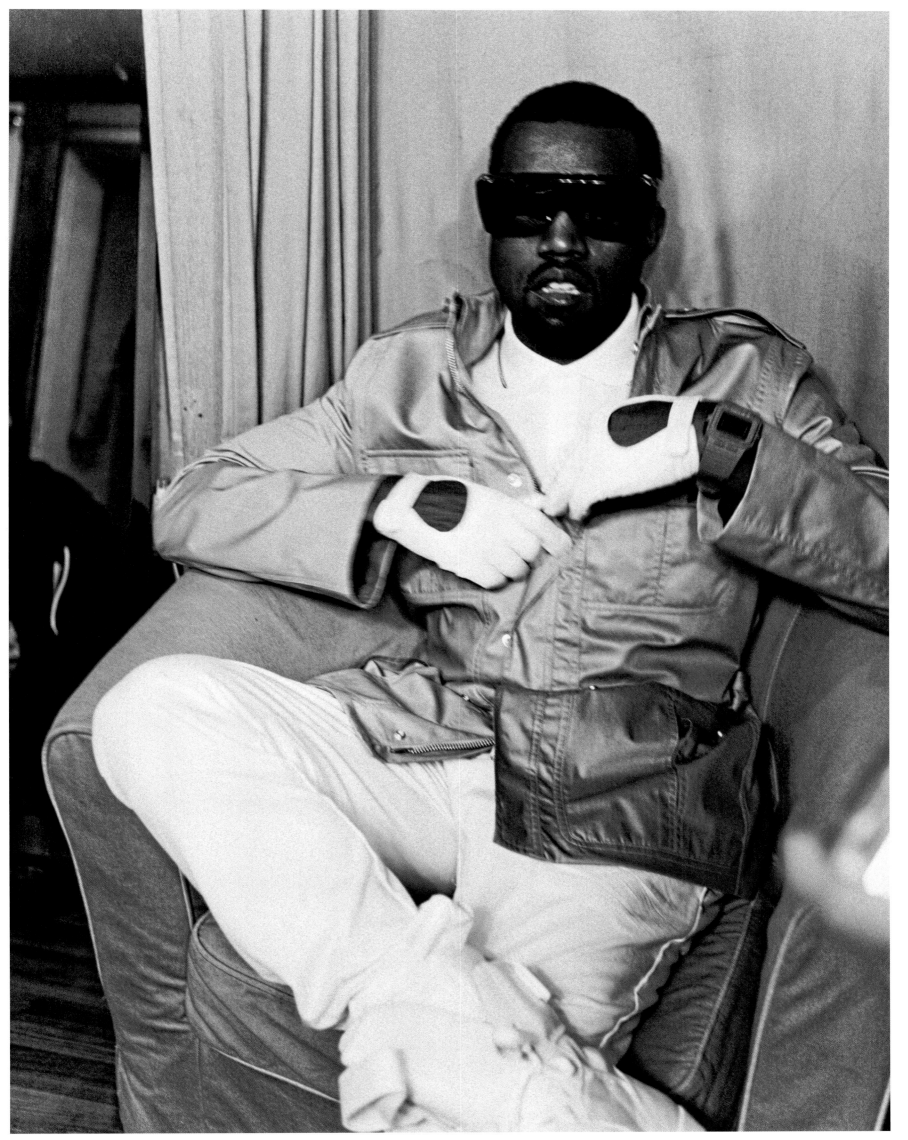

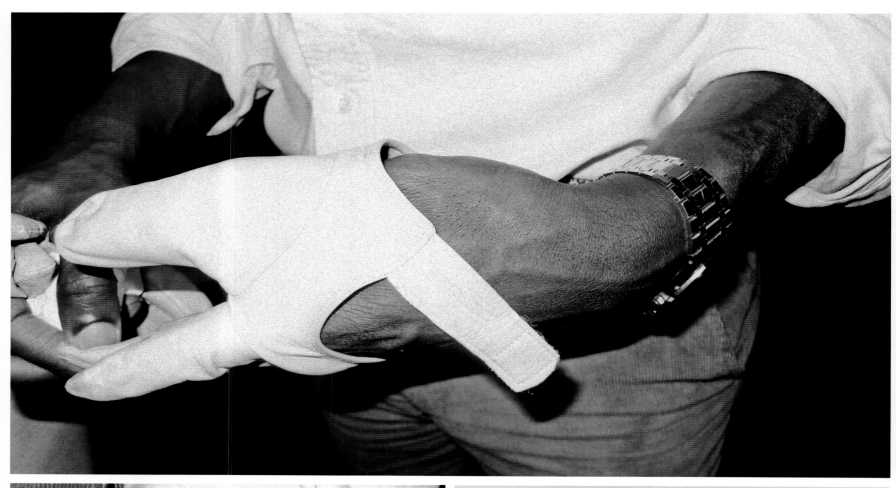

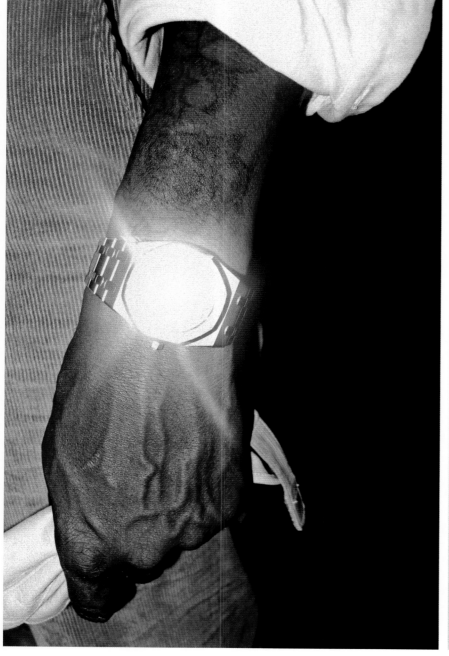

That's what life is about—naked alien chicks.

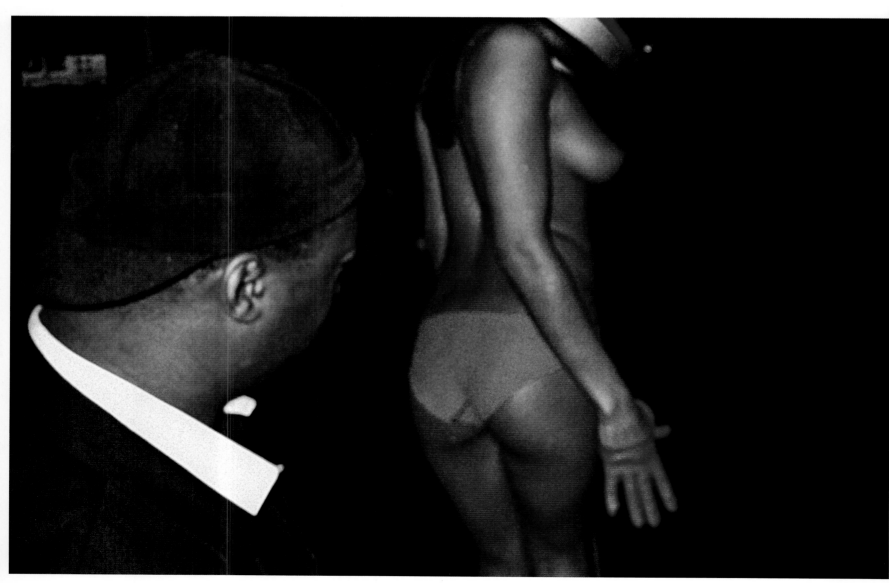

RIGHT Reading a review of the tour.

31ST BIRTHDAY PARTY

Let's talk about your porn, because you're really into porn. Do you watch porn every day? How much?

Every day.

When you wake up in the morning?

No, no, no, not every day that I wake up.

How often?

Three days out of the week.

You travel with porn?

Yeah, and I had to just re-up on some porn because, on my last world tour, I hadn't bought porn in, like, three or four months. I had to travel to Japan, China, and all these places where I could get in trouble if it's not a certain type of porn, if it doesn't have censors on it, meaning regular, penis-into-vagina porn, because they blur certain stuff in other countries. I remember I was going with this one girl in Australia. I said I bought some porn, and I was, like, "Man, this porn was so wack, because they'd be about to do the scene, then they'd cut! I'm, like, 'Wait a second. They didn't show the girl giving head!' And she's, like, 'That's good. It's good it had a little sensor on it.' I'm, like, 'You wack-ass bitch.'" [Laughter.]

What's your prerogative? Why are you talking bad about her? She's going to read this book and get her feelings hurt.

I had *my* feelings hurt when she didn't agree with me. [Laughter.]

This was the coolest birthday ever. To have a combination of Snoop—first of all, I had the absolute coolest people on the planet at my party, but, once Snoop is in the house, it gets even cooler. Then this douche with a capital BAG [pointing to picture of Jonze] shows up.

Editor: What is that [around Spike's head, opposite page]?

It's a Patrón wrapper from the Patrón bottle we drank on the way to the show.

These pictures are so great because this is the night of the party. It was really emotional for me because it represented all these different types of personalities...

L.A.—everybody was there. That's so great your birthday happened to be in L.A. How far into the tour is this? Still early on, right?

No, no, no. This is approaching the end of the tour.

This was a tour highlight? You felt like returning for more?

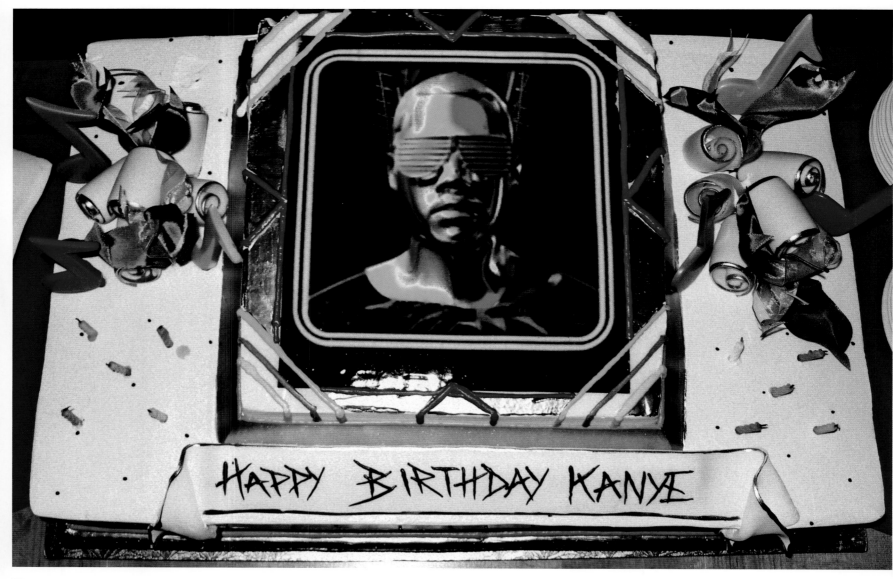

"**Kanye, I hope you and your dumbass spaceship Jane learn a lesson.**"
spinmagazine blogpost

"**Angry fans at the festival chanted 'Kanye sucks' and pelted the stage with empty glow sticks.**"
bbc.com

The Sun Exposes Kanye's Glow in the Dark Show
stereogum.com

Kanye Booed at Bonnaroo
E! Online

"**...it was going to be one of the highlights of my year (well other than shaking hands with Barack Obama).**"
kanyeuniversity.com message board

Kanye West Gets Blasted at Bonnaroo
celebuzz.com

Kanye West Rankles Bonnaroo with Tardy Pre-Dawn Set
rollingstone.com

Kanye West Screws Bonnaroo
allieiswired!.com

Kanye Blames Bonnaroo, Pearl Jam for 4:30 A.M. Show
mtv.com

Bonnaroo Crowd Tells Kanye West He Sucks
msnbc.com

Bonnaroo: Kanye West is an "Expletive Deleted"
postchronicle.com

After his set, the crowd chanted, "Kanye sucks!"
nytimes.com

Late Kanye not Feeling the Love at Bonnaroo Festival
efluxmedia.com

Winehouse Calls

...nye West

"C--t"

usmagazine.com

...d Kanye West Gig
...s Bonnaroo Crowd

foxnews.com

...ye West

...ngers

...ippies

gawker.com

...Kanye West
...Apologizes
...r Bonnaroo...
Sort of

dose.com

— Bonnaroo

...UCH!

...o6studios.com

...Fans Anger
...est is Late

...e.com

"Fuck Kanye West":
The Bonnaroo
Graffiti Photo Set

stereogum.com

"FUCK
KANYE
WEST

was heard from
all quarters."

thejtrain.com

Where Rock Lives:
Kanye's Bonnaroo Troubles

wnew.com

Delayed
Kanye West
Gig Angers
Bonnaroo Crowd

usatoday.com

Bonnaroo Crowd

Turns on

Kanye West

fasterlouder.com

"Robert Randolph,
the gospel slide guitarist,
came dangerously close to
cussing as he complained
about Mr. West."

nytimes.com

Kan...
Bonnar...

"...
S...

"This just makes
me sad. Kanye is
my homeboy."

kanyeuniversity.com message board

"I thought K...
was a douche...
Bonnaroo an...
through the s...

bonnaroo.com message...

"Grow...
Kany...

spinmagazine blog...

"...
g...
s...
d...

Damn You Pearl J...
You Ruined Bonn...
For Kanye!

therockdose.com

Wake Up
Bonnaro...
Mr. West...
Fuming!

americansongwriter.com

MANCHESTER, TENNESSEE
06.14.2008

BONNAROO MUSIC FESTIVAL

Kanye vs. Bonnaroo

douchebagface.com

W

"That night, Kanye West didn't go on until 4:15 AM upsetting what seemed like every single person at Bonnaroo. That's a lot of upset fans."

teenvogue.com blogpost

"Everyone could be heard mocking the rapper's actions during the final day of Bonnaroo."

wnew.com

KANYE SUCKS!

facebook.com

string
Kanye
ents.

Kanye Ate it! And Barfed it All Up!

perezhilton.com

Where Rock Lives: Kanye's Bonnaroo Troubles

wnew.com

I'll Be Honored By Kanye's Lateness

divertedmotion.com

es,
really
ye.

Kanye West Doesn't Care About White People

atlantasportsfan.com

you are
ntment."

s blogpost

Kanye's Bonnaroo Beef: a Fan's Guide

bigshotmag.com

morning I woke up and I felt to voice my disappointment in for Kanye's attitude and nce. I'm not saying I'll stop ing to his music or that dn't try to see him again at I don't want him to ut another album..."

thegrip.wordpress.com

"...that arrogant primadonna came on at about 4:30..."

kanyeuniversity.com message board

Kanye Flips Out

buzzfeed.com

Kanye West's Bonnaroo Debacle

spinmagazineonline.com

est Angers:
udience Chants
anye
cks"

Kanye Pisses
Bonnarooers off,
Offers Shoe
as Compensation.

consequenceofsound.com

He did
Kanye's sho
for Kanye.

heraldtimes.com

tonpost.com

ore
pt
."

"Kanye made no friends
at Bonnaroo
and that's hard to
accomplish."

pastemagazine.com

Kanye West Earn
Haters at Bonnar

spinner.com

up
"

"I can almost assure you that
when 2:45 rolled around his
ass was still in Atlanta."

kanyeuniversity.com message board

Another in a
of recent K
'me' mome

wnew.com

e's no reason to
cist here. Kanye's
ng had nothing to
th his skin color."

yeuniversity.com message board

Kanye Acts like a
Jackass
Again.

soupytrumpet.com

No gues
appearan
just a really,
tardy Kan

thegrip.wordpress.com

The Great Bonnaroo
Kanye West
Disaster of '08

thejtrain.com

"Kanye,
a disappo

spinmagazine

"I can't believe I missed
Talib Kweli to wait
for this…"

kanyeuniversity.com message board

"The next
obligated
and disda
performa
lister
I woul
or th
put

Kanye West
Keeps Bonnaroo
Fans Waiting
Until 4:25A.M.

digg.com

Also,
WHAT
the %#@* was
he wearing?!

spinmagazine blogpost

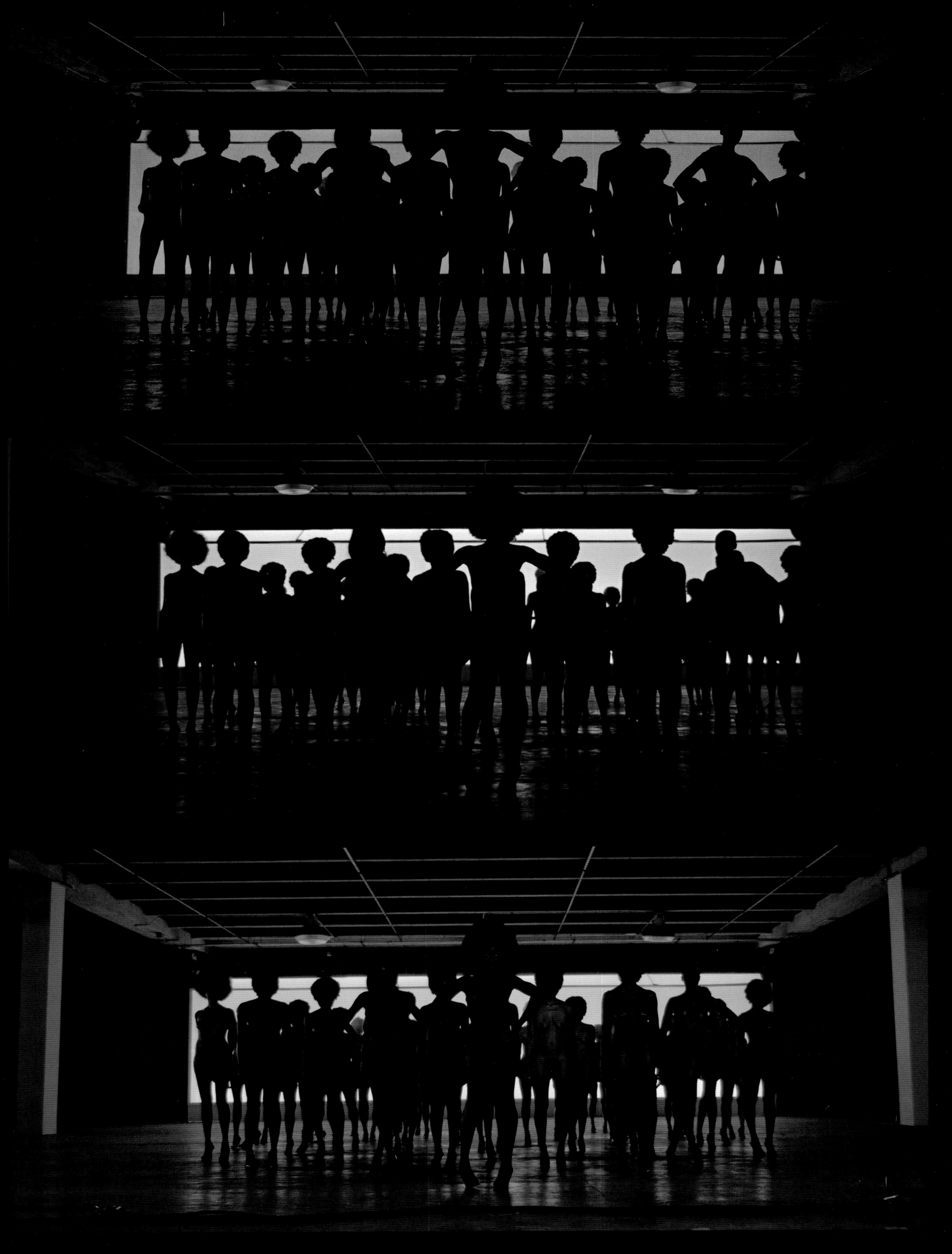

VANESSA BEECROFT
808S & HEARTBREAK LISTENING PARTY

"I was raised in Italy with no TV, no radio, no telephone, no car, no motorbike, no pop music, no Coca-Cola, no Barbie dolls. I have yet a lot to catch up with.

When Kanye contacted me I was fascinated by his world but ignorant. What his world may be missing is equal to what I am missing from mine and this encounter is refreshing. It is not conventional because neither world knows how to operate in the other one. I also interpret this encounter as an encounter between genders and race, and strongly support it. When we worked together Kanye had a clear visual expectation and art references he was aiming for. My musical references were Wagner, Arvo Pärt, and Philip Glass. So I utilized the environment he provided, as I usually do with architecture, and installed the girls there to fight that situation in the same way they would fight a museum or a gallery."

—Vanessa Beecroft

Before we went on the second leg of the Glow in the Dark tour, we had a listening party for my new album that I had decided to fucking record in the midst of when I'm touring, and release. So I had a listening session with Vanessa Beecroft, the performance artist, who's well known for taking nudes and having them stand in one place.

Look how happy you are [below image]: "This is my favorite day ever!"

And why would I be happy around a bunch of naked women? [Laughter.]

How did you get familiar with her work?

She did some stuff with Louis Vuitton. Her work is just so impactful. Her images—you see certain images, and it just evokes a certain, not emotion, but music score—a still that evokes a score. Her stills evoke scores.

They just stood in place as you played the whole record? Did they ever move?

They do whatever they feel like, and start crying, they sit down, different people are doing different things. The event was like a brain fuck; people were, like, "I don't know what to think. I can't grasp that."

Where was it?

It was in L.A., just down the street. It was, once again, a culmination of culture, all types of cool people—Rick Ross, Michael Rappaport, Jeremy Scott, and Jay-Z were all there.

TOP LEFT Me and Vanessa Beecroft. TOP RIGHT Me at the mixing board. BOTTOM Me about to enter the models' dressing room.

This is Glow in the Dark Asia: "Stand in line." All this military stuff, getting searched, looking through stuff, looking through your computer.

You lived in China for a bit when you were a kid?

I stayed in China for a year. Me and my mom. She was an English professor. I was ten years old.

Do you know any Chinese?

Just hello, goodbye.

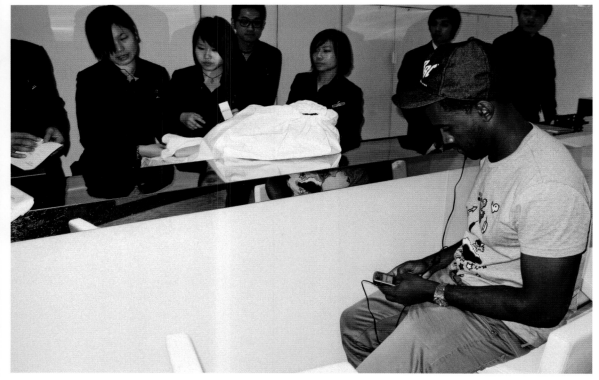

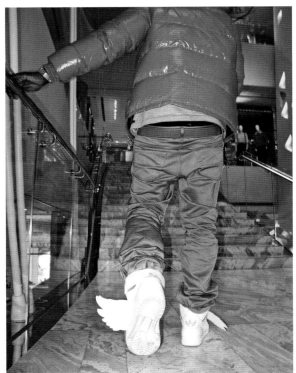

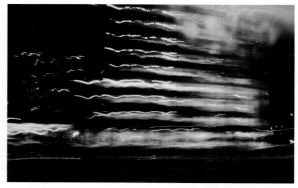

[Talking about images on following spread.] I love these photos because they remind me of _Lost in Translation_.

Where is this?

This is in Singapore at a press conference for _808s & Heartbreak_. I think it's an arrogant statement for me to compare myself to you, but I think we are like the music and director counterparts, having avant-garde ideas that are successful and people being envious of you. People will be talking shit and it's, like, "I'm sorry that people liked it. I'm planning on doing something good again." I say it's similar because you'll have, like, a really, really cool idea, but it will also be a really, really pop idea. Like when—who is the King of New York? What's his name?

Christopher Walken.

Yeah, that fucking Christopher Walken dancing? I like that even better than the one where you were dancing, because I like high production value, I'm kind of glossy—I love that video. I felt like it should've won. But for me, for my brand, I think my brand has a bit of high production—

You want it to look like money—

If I went and did a tour right now, people would be, like, "We came to Kanye West to get the Louis Vuitton of shows."

Don't you think that...that won't always apply? This record is really stripped down—you wouldn't tour _808s & Heartbreak_ the same way you toured this record, would you?

No. My idea for _808s & Heartbreak_ is to start off with a mike stand and a spotlight, and you hear the footsteps, and I just walk up to the mike, which is completely different than fucking crash-landing on a planet, but still, at a certain point, it'll take you all the way to like full-on fabric's flying, and Tycos, and motherfuckers doing karate in the garage, or whatever. That's the way I think my record is. I think it's very minimal, like "Love Lockdown"— you could've almost did that in your basement [sings]. Actually, Sam [Spiegel, Spike's brother] gave me that 808.

He gave you the actual 808?

The actual 808 sound. Sam gave me that sound. It's like a dirty, fucked-up 808, and inspired me to go [sings baseline of song], and I just did the song in five minutes [sings baseline again]. It's very lo-fi, and I actually sang kind of off-pitch and put it out like that to act like I was an independent artist, where it didn't even matter if it was on pitch or not, like trying to be Cody Chestnutt—to completely just press RESET. That was the idea. But by the end of the day, songs like "Robocop" and "Paranoia"—I just can't help it. I like to produce shit and take it to that world. I think that's what will happen with the next tour. It will eventually go to some over-the-top place.

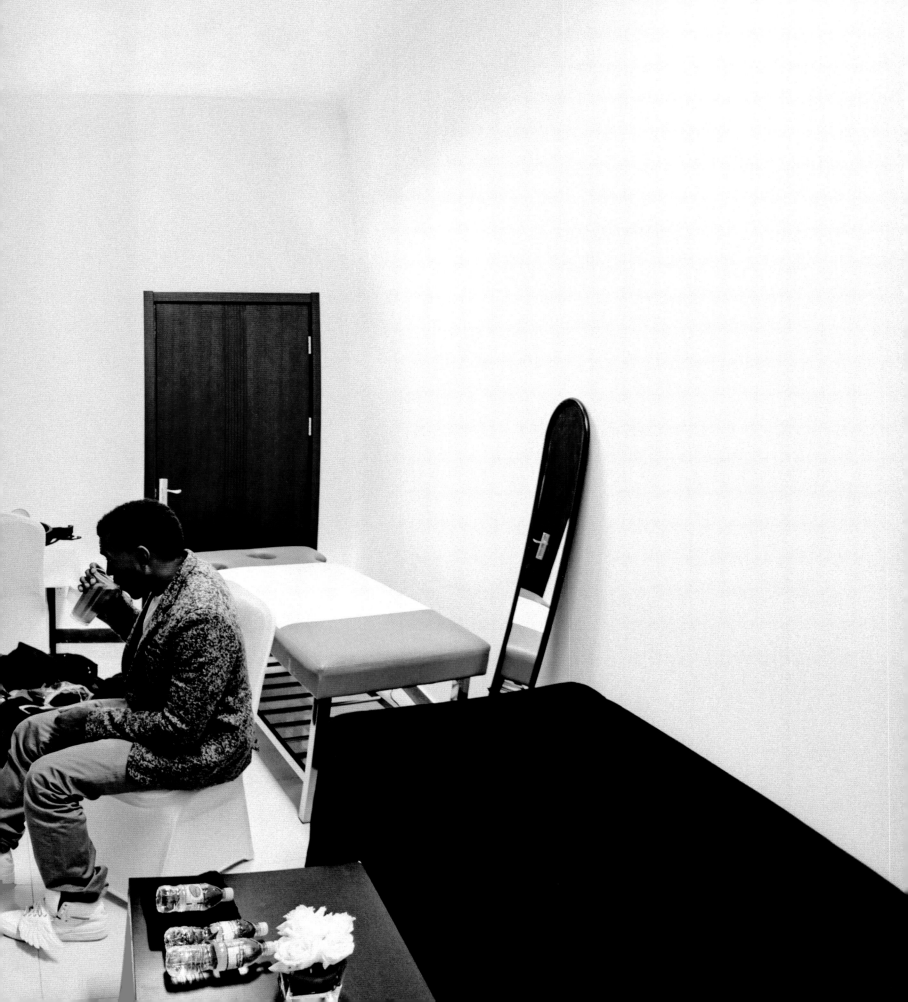

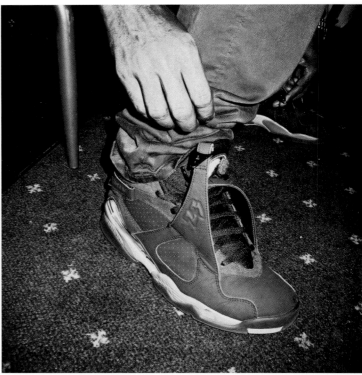

[Previous spread] I thought this shot was so Kubrick-meets-, like, supermess. Look how stark that room is. This best describes what the fuck is going on before I hit the stage.

It's just you and some anonymous woman.

That's my wardrobe person, waters, a towel, and some tea.

Nobody around. Before you went on, did you always take twenty minutes where you wouldn't see anyone?

No, I'd usually be talking to my friends, because we really are in the fucking army. At a certain point it was, like, "I *just* saw you, just now. I look at you every single day of my life. What's new? Man, you remember back when Acura was a good car? When you could get pussy off an Acura?" [Laughter.] That'd be a conversation. This is me lacing the Jordans up, about to hit the stage, lights—crazy outfit, in my personal opinion. You might not agree with me. You might not be into the whole red pants, leopard jacket, and white T-shirt look.

I haven't really rocked that lately, that look.

MTV EUROPE AWARDS

[Previous spread] Where was this?

The MTV Europe Awards. I just won an award. "Thank you," acting like a bitch—not like a bitch, but just not boisterous or happy.

Not grateful at all?

I was grateful. I just didn't want to say anything wrong, so I was just mad, acting kind of programmed, like, [sounding like a robot] "I just want to thank everyone."

Why? Were you going through a period where you didn't want to say anything that was going to get you in trouble?

Yeah, like I had probably just dealt with a whole bunch of press coming in with a bunch of weird-ass quotes and people taking stuff out of context and making me look like a complete monster. [Imitating press person.] "Do not sound like a monster." [Sounding like a monster.] "Thank you!"

[This spread] **This was in an airport when we landed in Germany, and Barack is getting elected president. It was, like, "What the fuck?" We were on a plane, and this is us going crazy in the airport looking at the screen. Look at everybody's face!**

That's amazing. Who's that there?

That's D.J. Craze in the shiny jacket.

What was your reaction when he got elected president? What was your first thought?

It was like that T-Pain song [sings]: "I can't believe it." That was a theme song, and we still can't believe it to this day. I can't wait until [inaugural] Tuesday. Oh, my God.

Are you going to the inauguration?

I'm going to perform. It's going to be the shit.

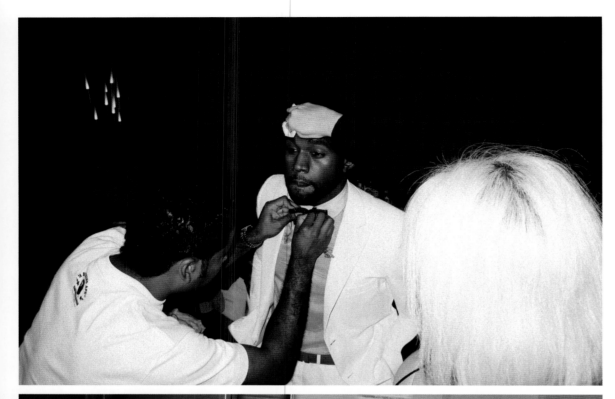

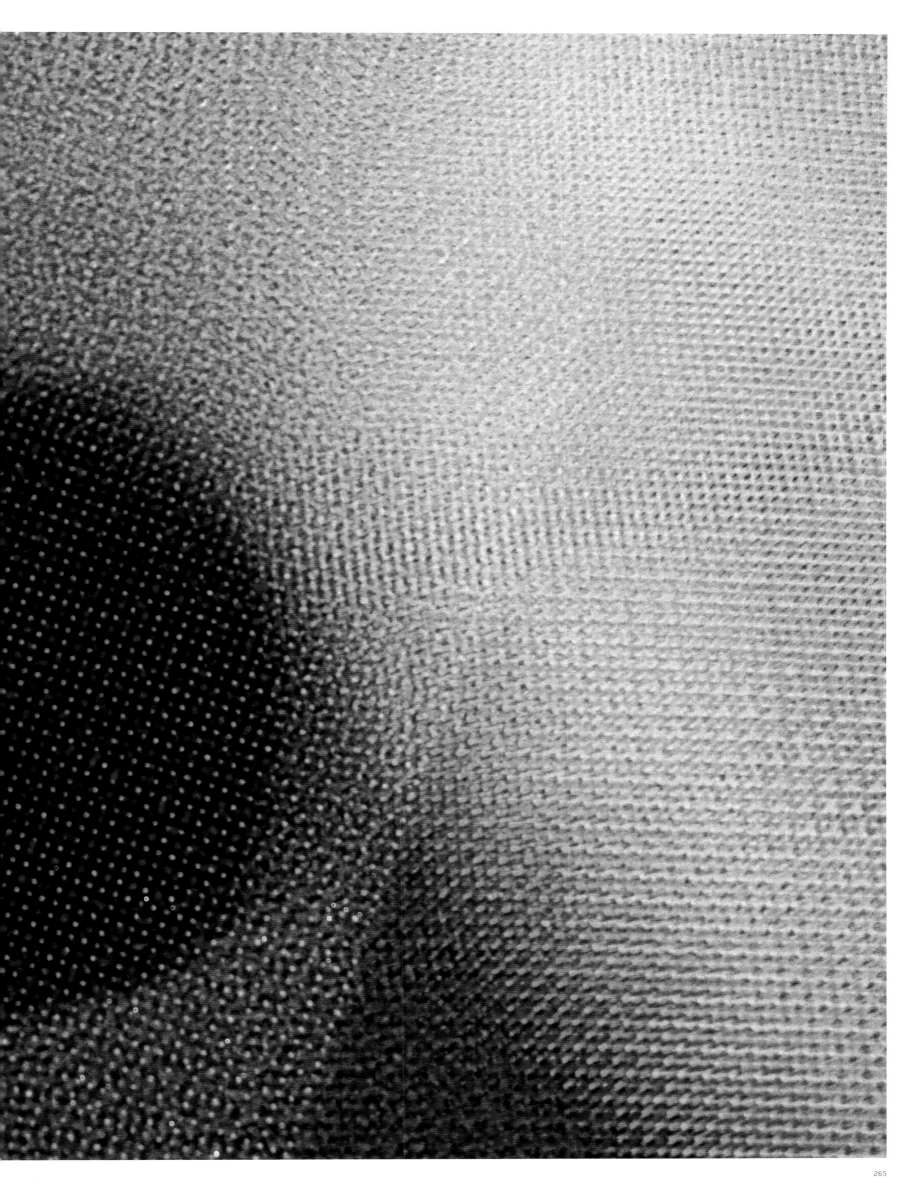

This is the MTV Europe Awards backstage. This is us backstage. Look at this.

Paul McCartney. Had you met him before?

At an awards show.

Was it good to meet him? "I'm hugging a Beatle." [Laughter.]

That's Mr. Hudson, one of my artists. Look how dope his fucking jacket is. Paul McCartney and

Beyoncé with the glove. Look at this shit. This is what the fuck I'm talking about. This is what pop is right now. Look at his jacket. Look at her glove. Get busy.

Wow. Where's that? [Next spread]

It's at the awards. We performed "American Boy," then they showed Barack really big on the screen.

THIS SPREAD, FROM LEFT TO RIGHT Estelle and Perez Hilton;
me and Estelle; Beyoncé; Bono; Lyor Cohen (CEO of Warner
Music Group, also one of the earliest heads of Def Jam);
Mr. Hudson playing a new song for me; Brandon Flowers of
The Killers; Sir Paul McCartney.

FOLLOWING SPREAD AND CLOSING IMAGES The 02 Arena in
London and onstage shots of performances in the U.K. the
second time around, with opening acts Mr. Hudson and the
Library, Syren, Estelle, and Santigold. I closed the tour in
Australia on 12.07.2008—where it began.

What country is this?

**London. [Sings] "Just touched down in London Town."
Look at us. Look at this scarf. We're going crazy. Look
at this cheetah coat. That's Santigold. That's Mr.
Hudson right there. Look at his outfit, red pants. That's
his group right there. Look at that. We're going crazy.**

We're out of our minds licking those steps. Will.i.am. That's Big Sean, one of my artists. This is Kid Cudi, and look, Nas is in the building. Mos Def.

What are you guys doing?

We're just doing rap, man. This is after the London show. The shit was *crazy*.

That was the last show?

That wasn't the very last show, but that was a culmination of all the energy.

It felt like the end, a big celebration. Think about this: when you're an old man, how are you going to look back at this year?

Like those shots that you saw with me in those crazy outfits. I'm going to be, like, "Man, we were cool. We were really fucking rock stars. We were out of our minds. We're walking around wearing that shit. We're going to look back, like, 'Yeah, we wore that shit on the streets. We were crazy.'" Hopefully I'll still be equally as crazy when I'm an old man.

**This is the shit that says we really lived it.
We were on some rock-and-roll shit.**

281

Don't dim your personality.